THE GREAT WALL OF US

Government Stealing From
Small Business. Run For Your
Life-Get Your Blind Fold Off

JOSEPH N. COOPER

outskirtspress
DENVER, COLORADO

Outskirts Press, Inc.
http://www.outskirtspress.com

ISBN: 978-1-4787-6495-3

Outskirts Press and the "OP" logo are trademarks belonging to Outskirts Press, Inc.

PRINTED IN THE UNITED STATES OF AMERICA

Acknowledgments

I wish to thank my mentor and dear friend James Schorr for his assistance in helping me bring this book to market. In addition, I want to thank Cheryleta Murphy for her strong, steady support.

Foreword

There are those who would suggest or say you cannot compare what happened to the Cherokee and J. Cooper & Associates Inc. JCA was a company and was mistreated by the Federal Government while the Cherokee who had their own language and alphabet were destroyed, not just mistreated.

The only comparison I am making, the Federal Government treated JCA and the Cherokee in the same manner. They stole from both parties. The Cherokee lost their land and the war, I lost my business and a great deal of money. That is the common connection, stealing. In stealing from JCA the Federal Government took contracts set aside for JCA and give those contracts to big companies claiming to be small contractors thereby committing fraud.

There isn't any question that the Federal Government ignored the rules it set-up. Is the desk stacked at GAO and the Court of Federal Claims against Small Business, you bet they are? There are many lawyers who have knowledge of the US Court of Federal Claims or have argued before the court who would not disagree with me that the court protects the Federal Government at all cost.

Contents

Author's Comments

Some months ago, I was talking to a really old and dear friend about my earlier book, *The Case,* which pointed out the very serious problem of federal government contracts designated by law for small and women- or minority-owned businesses being fraudulently given to large, multi-million dollar corporations.

During our talk, my friend, who was in the Smoky Mountains at the time, said "It's not new!" He started talking about the "Trail of Tears," and what happened to the Cherokee or Eastern Band of Cherokee, two centuries ago. At first, I didn't really catch his point, because I never heard much about the Trail of Tears. As he continued, I perked up when he pointed out the similar happenings the Cherokee and today's small businesses experience with government and its courts.

My issues dealt with my company losing federal government contracts that were legally set aside only for small business – but given to huge corporations, fraudulently misrepresenting themselves knowingly to the government as small businesses. The Cherokee had similar experiences with the federal government that small businesses encounter today.

The Cherokee experience dealt with wealthy European (Euro) farmers and settlers who wanted the Cherokee lands – and who had the money and power to get the government to do what they wanted. And, now 200 years later, huge corporations give millions of dollars to government officials and politicians – to get them to turn their heads, ignore the law, and steal government contracts set aside for small business.

My friend told me how the government lied and stole the land under several treaties the government set up for that purpose. Even more relevant for small businesses, he told me about the long legal battles the Cherokee went through – but even when they won their case, President Andrew Jackson refused to enforce the court's decision.

My friend told me about the public not knowing the truth about what the government was doing to the Cherokee – just as the public today has no idea of the truth about what the government is doing to cripple small businesses by stealing for their big-business benefactors.

The experience of my company, J. Cooper & Associates

Inc. (JCA), is a perfect example of the stealing from thousands of small businesses, estimated by the American Small Business League to be more than 100 billion dollars every year. It is shocking how federal bureaucrats and their own appointed courts can free-ly break congressional laws and contracts with small businesses – the same way they broke their promises and treaties with the Cherokee Nation.

In the case of small businesses, it deals with the bil-lions of dollars set aside for small businesses being taken away and given to huge corporations, with the federal government taking the lead in committing this fraud. Just like the Cherokee, my company spent more than fifteen years in our government court "system" to correct the wrong to no avail. Just like the Cherokee, laws already existed to protect my company – but government refused to enforce these laws.

I believe I have an important mission to tell and help millions of small businesses not to go through what I have gone through with our government. It is my hope that the reader can experience something good, learning from all of my agony – if you have a small business, the government is your worst imaginable customer! Run for your life, literally, when they insist you drop your private customers to give them more attention!

After my friend had finished talking to me about the Cherokee experience with the government and I realized how certain were similar experiences JCA encountered, I felt ashamed that I knew so little about the Cherokee and the Trail of Tears, and how our government treated these people. I decided that I would learn as much as I can about this matter.

CHAPTER 1

Private and Public Power – Economic Power vs. Political

Influence on Small Business Set-Aside Contracts

(President Jackson, 200 years ago and the government today understands the difference between private and public power and economic power vs. political.)

> *"[E]nsuring small businesses can thrive is about more than economic success. It's also about who we are as a people. It's about a nation where anybody who's got a good idea and a willingness to work hard can succeed. That's the central promise of America."*
>
> -President Barack Obama

Small businesses are leaders in innovation and drivers of the economy. Small businesses hold more patents than all of the nation's universities and largest corporations combined, and create two- thirds of all private sector jobs, employing half of all working Americans.

The federal government is the largest buyer in the world, spending over $500 billion each year. For the federal government, contracting with small businesses is common sense. Small businesses get the revenue they need to create jobs and drive the economy forward, and federal agencies get the creativity; but when small businesses are excluded from federal contracts, the federal government, American taxpayers, and the nation's economy lose out.

Over thirty years ago, Congress set a goal of having a certain portion of all federal contracting dollars go to small businesses and established sub-goals for small businesses owned by women, socially and economically disadvantaged individuals, and service-disabled veterans of the Armed Forces, and for small businesses in Historically Underutilized Business Zones (HUBZones). The current government-wide goal for small businesses' share of contracting dollars is 23%. Every year since 2006, the federal government has missed the 23% small business goal and all but one of the sub-goals; the 2009 shortfall was greater than $4 billion. Removing barriers to federal contracting and increasing access for small businesses will go a long way toward closing this gap. It is important that small businesses understand the differences among private and public power, economic power vs. political power, and their influence on small business.

There is an incredible disparity in economic, private, and public power in a political world that is troubled. It was this way 200 years ago when the Cherokee and other tribes was fighting the US Government, to keep their homeland. The difference between political power and other social power between government and the private organization is, Government holds a legal control on the use of physical force.

This is the problem that small business contractors are facing today in obtaining federal government contracts that have been set aside by the government for their use. It is also the problem that small businesses have when seeking favorable rulings from the courts and other government agencies responsible for resolving disputes between small businesses and government.

Like the Cherokee Indians, small businesses all pursued help from the courts and Congress, only to be turned away. A typical small business contractor represents one vote when attempting to bring about change. That one vote is an important political tool. I think it is safe to say that often this small contractor is overwhelmed by well-organized big business campaigns involving their lobbies. In contrast, for a corporate executive, his vote is the least-important political tool. His political influence is much more effective by donating thousands of dollars to political action committees and individual candidates, all working to help his favorite politicians who intern will help him obtain government contracts and other favors.

Some people and big businesses have big financial resources that they can turn into political influence-- which they do. It happened over two hundred years ago with the Cherokee and it is happening today with big businesses taking away contracts set aside for small businesses. Small business contractors cannot possibly conduct campaigns like big businesses because they don't have the money and resources. We have two citizens, the contractor and company executive, who are supposed to be equal from a political point of view, but they have major differences in their amount of power.

I am not certain that many small business contractors fully understand the imbalance in private and public influence and how it works within our government. In bringing about change and fixing the problems small contractors are having, with obtaining contracts set aside for them, they must understand how private economic power works and how easily it becomes public political power. They must also understand how the federal government protects itself and will do whatever is necessary to hold on to its power, even if that means ignoring and breaking the laws.

The American government is now increasingly responsive to special interests and not the public interest. Clearly, this is why many Americans are frustrated and disappointed with our political system. Instead of a democracy where all citizens have an equal say in the governing process, some organizations and individuals have a disproportionate and unfair influence over what the government does. The result is that the power and greed of the few too often win out over the needs of the many. The prime example is what small business contractors are going through today. Large contractors are working closely with government contracting officers in redirecting contracts set aside for small contractors to big businesses claiming to be small businesses, and the government does nothing about it, though they know that laws are being broken.

There are many ways that private power is being turned into public power. It involves a great deal of money. Money is the most available and flexible form of power, because it can buy so many different forms of political influence. The Cherokee Indians found out this fact while fighting for their land in Georgia over 200 years ago. White farmers had the money to greatly influence government that had the political power to control the land and its people. Today, small business contractors are experiencing a similar fate to that which the Cherokee went through 200 years ago.

I have tried to make clear that all in our world is not what we've been told. The older I get, the more I see how we have been deceived on such a grand scale that if most people knew, we would have a difficult time comprehending its full extent.

Our government cannot lie successfully to us, if not for the media's full cooperation. The media is a critical part of ensuring the government's success. The behind the scenes of big money and politics are so well hidden from the public that if the public actually knew how things really work, we would have a revolution. I read someplace that Henry Ford once said: "It is well enough that people of the nation do not understand our banking and monetary system, for if they did, I believe there would be a revolution before tomorrow morning."

Our politicians will lie to the public in a heartbeat if it means getting what they want. What most people don't have a clue about is that the media lies and deceives us just as much, if not more--I can't stress enough the importance of small business contractors understanding what I am talking about and getting involved to try and correct the problem. How the media works with big business is a perfect example of how money is used for both private and public power. Another example of how big business makes use of money that is worth mentioning is that in 1917 Congressman Oscar Callaway, documented in official Congressional Record (US Record, Vol 54, date 02/09/1917), that millionaire Morgan, infiltrated the US media for the sole purpose of controlling it. Morgan hired twelve news managers to help him determine the most influential newspapers in America. JP Morgan's efforts were successful.

The less responsive the government and Congress are to the small business contract set-aside question, the less likely it is that they will act in the small business contractor's interest. A great many Americans are tired of our government lying to them, not telling the truth, and not caring what the people think or want. The government has continued to lie for years, telling the people that they are not giving contracts set aside for small businesses to big businesses. There is no question that there is a perception that the government is working for a few, and not the many. I believe it is part of the reason for the public hostility toward politicians and government. Many Americans have been blindfolded for many years by the lying of our government, and only as we get older do we see the truth and realize what our government has been telling us these many years are lies.

There will be some who will say I am cynical about our government who consistently favor special interests over the public or small business contractor. I feel I have very little say over what our government does, and I see how our government works for special interests. It is only natural for me to be distrustful of the institution. I, like many Americans, wonder just who really is influencing what government does. A clear majority of us now think the government is run by a few big business interests looking out for themselves.

It is easy to lay blame for our unresponsive public institutions on politicians and the government itself; however, this would be a mistake. Bad government is just the symptom. This problem ultimately is a political illness which has its roots in society at large in the private sector. The problem is private economic power, mainly money that is not distributed equally among all citizens. There are those in our society, organizations and individuals, who have very big financial resources that they can turn into political influence. Equally, private economic power too easily becomes public political power. This is what is hurting the whole small business set-aside contract question. Small contractors must understand this issue if they hope to bring about change. In order for small business contractors to be equal, political power must be shared.

It is very important that small business contractors fight

for political power. Government would then respond favorably to what the contractors want—we would see one vote for the contractor and one vote for the executive. In looking at how private power becomes public power, one must look at large sums of money. Money can buy almost anything. Most importantly, it can buy many different forms of political influence. It can buy lobby companies, political candidates, information, and much more. We need to work toward making our voices heard, making ourselves equal to big business. Today we are not equal. Big business contractors are well-organized to get government to give them what they want. We must strive toward this objective if we are to see a difference. Life teaches us many lessons--it stands to reason that the longer we live, the more lessons we learn.

CHAPTER 2

Legal Review
ᎣᏂᏪᎵ ᎠᏍᎦᏅᎢ

Two hundred years ago the Cherokee, under the leadership of Chief Ross, sought out help from the courts for the Cherokee to keep their land in Georgia. He believed in the American legal system and insisted that the Cherokee go through the system. In his case before the Supreme Court, he won the legal victory, but lost the war when President Jackson refused to enforced the court decision.

Today, many in our country would argue that the relationship with the federal government over the years with the Cherokee and Indian tribes is chock-full of a number of examples of brutalities and shameful actions on the part of our government toward the Indians over the years.

Like Ross, I too believed in the America legal system until I went through it with my case. It took me many years to learn and understand that I could not possibly have received an objective hearing from the US Court of Federal Claims regarding my case against the federal government. Before I could start my argument before the court, my case was dead on arrival.

> *"It is as much the duty of government to render prompt justice against itself in favor of citizens, as it is to administer the same, between private individuals."*

> - Abraham Lincoln.

Questions:
Is There Justice in the US Court of Federal Claims?

The US Court of Federal Claims is one of two federal institutions designed to provide for the determination of private claims against the United States Government. The other government institution designed to handle disputes with the federal government is GAO. Between the court of Federal Claims and GAO, it is very difficult for a small contractor to obtain justice or win a protest.

The US Court of Federal Claims is integrally related to the fundamental principle of the US Constitution that individuals have rights against the government. The court traces its origins directly back to 1855, when Congress established the United States Court of Claims to provide for the determination of private claims against the United States.

If you are a small business with grievances against the federal government, bringing your case before the US Court of Federal Claims to seek justice will give you an eye-opener in disbelief. You must be prepared to accept losing your case no matter how well-intentioned your case may be. You must be prepared to accept that the court is the first line of defense to protect the federal government's illegal policies and behavior. The federal government is defended by the US Court of Federal Claims.

I took my case to the US Court of Federal Claims, for justice. It did not occur to me that I would not receive an objective hearing. I and my lawyers were very optimistic given the evidence and facts of my case. The US Court of Federal Claims, which hears all claims against the government, also "finds" in favor of the government in the majority of the cases it "hears."

There is no question that the US Court of Federal Claims protects the government against plaintiff filing action against the government. <u>Over 97% of the court rulings favored the US Government</u>. Between 1% and

3% favored the plaintiffs. These numbers need no explanation they are self-explanatory. It truly is unbelievable that these numbers can be so high and low. One could suggest that the US Federal Claims Court is "The Great Wall of US," in the manner they decide their cases protecting the government.

When you think of the volume of cases before the court each year, it is hard to understand how the public could receive a fair hearing. One could ask the question "Why bring your case to the US Court of Federal Claims for justice when it is clear the chance of winning is very remote?" The majority of Americans have never heard of this these numbers.

According to the court of Federal Claims, in 2006 there were 8,724 cases on the court docket involving more than 10,000 plaintiffs; of these, 3,091 cases involved the court's general jurisdiction, while 5,633 are vaccine cases handled, in the first instance, by the court's special masters.

Many of the cases on the court's docket are particularly complex and seek large damage awards:

A. The general jurisdiction non-pro se cases pending before the court during 2006 include damage claims in excess of $197 billion.

B. In 2006, the court rendered judgments in

more than 900 cases and awarded $1.8 bil-
lion in damages. Less Than 1%.

In 2012, the US Court of Federal Claims reported:

Amount claimed in fiscal year   46,408,652,000
2012 fillings

Amount awarded in judgments for   810,147,115
plaintiffs / petitioners

Amount awarded in judgments for   22,026,849
plaintiffs carrying interest

It is clear when reviewing the US Federal Court of
Claims awards for 2006, one could understand why
small businesses cannot expect a fair hearing from the
court of Claims.

When taking your dispute to court, remember, try to
maintain one mindset, isolate the issues, and bring the
matter to conclusion. The civil justice system is much
like it was 200 years ago. If dealing with simple or complex matters, it could take a long time and cost in the
thousands of dollars. At this point it would no longer
serve as an effective tool in regulating society's legal
matters. The system is clearly dysfunctional; it is practi-
cally impossible for the average person to rely on getting
justice or resolving a dispute in the court system.

When one looks at 97% of the US Court of Federal

Claims rulings in favor of the US Government and 1% - 2% in favor of the plaintiff, it doesn't take much to see the truth.

An Overview of the United States Court of Federal Claims

- Established by Congress in 1855 as the court of Claims, the court was reorganized by Congress in 1982 as the United States Court of Federal Claims. In general, the court is entrusted with exclusive, nationwide jurisdiction over various money claims against the United States in excess of $10,000. The court hears suits involving government contracts, Constitutional claims, tax refunds, Indian claims, civilian and military pay claims, patent and copyright matters, and vaccine injury claims. Congress also has authorized the court to review agency decisions under various federal compensation programs. In addition, the court has the unique authority within the federal judiciary to advise Congress, when requested, on private relief bills. The rationale for the court remains as it has been over the past 150 years: to fulfill the need for a national court that can handle cases throughout the country and develop a uniform of body of law in critical subject areas.

- The Court of Federal Claims has had exclusive jurisdiction since 2001 to enter judgment in government contract cases. The previous concurrent jurisdiction with federal district courts was eliminated by Congress, in large part because of the need for a uniform body of law and a national court that could hold hearings throughout the country. *See* 142 Cong. Rec. S11848-01 (1996). Consistent with this need for a uniform body of law, Congress has also given the court exclusive jurisdiction over claims under the National Childhood Vaccine Injury Act of 1986, as amended.

- During 2006, there were 8,724 cases on the court's docket, involving more than 10,000 plaintiffs. Of these, 3,091 cases involve the court's general jurisdiction, while 5,633 are vaccine cases handled, in the first instance, by the court's special masters.

- In keeping with the criteria used by the federal district courts in calculating their caseloads based on the number of authorized judgeships, in 2006, the court of Federal Claims had 193 cases for each of its 16 authorized judgeships (taking into account only the general jurisdiction docket).

- Many of the cases on the court's docket are particularly complex and seek large damage awards:

» The general jurisdiction non-pro se cases pending before the court during 2006 include damage claims in excess of $197 billion.

» In 2006, the court rendered judgments in more than 900 cases and awarded $1.8 billion in damages.

» Over 60% of the Fortune 100 companies have been parties in cases before the court. Many have been a party on more than one occasion.

▪ Examples of some of the cases that are being handled (or have recently been handled) by the court illustrate the complexity, diversity and significance of the court's docket:

» A series of approximately 120 contract cases, referred to collectively as *Winstar* cases, involving the collapse of the savings and loan industry in the 1980s and the legislation enacted by Congress in response to the collapse. The Justice Department, at one point, estimated that those cases involved dollar claims of more than $30 billion and over a billion pages of documents.

Is This Justice?

SGᎪᏅᎰᎠᎪ ᎠᏔᎢ?

I believe that my problems in obtaining justice in the US Court of Federal Claims system started with the decision of Judge Marian Blank Horn. My lawyer and I argued in the court of Federal Claims that the INS had not operated in good faith when it stopped giving JCA work on the INS contract.

The INS said it was not satisfied with JCA's work and the cost associated with it. But in a deposition, Joseph Garforth, a senior INS contacting officer at the agency, said no evidence was ever offered to him questioning the quality of JCA's work. A government audit, which was paid for by INS, found that the cost was actually reasonable.

Still, the court sided with the INS and said that because the agency had given JCA the minimum amount on the contract, there was no evidence the agency had not operated in good faith. JCA appealed the ruling, but an appeals court upheld the lower court ruling.

There were numerous existing legislative and regula-tions and executive remedies that could address JCA's concern already on the books showing where the gov-ernment broke existing laws. The only decision Judge

Horn had to execute was to ask why SBA did not enforce the law. The FAR regulations and SBA policies and regulations, which do fall under US Court of Federal Claims jurisdiction, clearly supported JCA's argument. Judge Horn could have recognized the Department of Justice IG Investigative Report, dated August 1977, which confirmed that contractors misrepresented their small business status in order to acquire contracts set aside for JCA.

JCA clearly demonstrated to the US Court of Federal Claims that, under the common law of contracts, the government had breached its contractual duty of good faith and fair dealing, where the INS program and contracting officials either knew or had reason to know that JCA's competitors had falsely certified themselves as small, disadvantaged businesses—yet the INS officials continued to contract with those competitors, to JCA's detriment.

The crucial issue placed before the Claims Court was whether the INS's conduct in this case constituted a breach of contract under federal contract law. The court, in turn, relied upon the questionable, but often cited, proposition that, in order to demonstrate that the government failed to act in good faith, the contractor must prove that the government acted in *"bad faith."* Under the *"bad faith"* standard, the contractor must show *"irrefragable proof"* that the government official acted with specific disposition against the contractor—a virtually impossible standard to meet. However, I believe the evidence and facts in my case met this burden.

"PROCUREMENT LAW ADVISOR:

Volume 8, Issue 9
December 2005

Court of Federal Claims Gives Last Rites to "Irrefragable Proof" Standard

ADVISORY: In a series of recent decisions, the U.S. Court of Federal Claims has eroded the proof necessary to defeat to the oft-invoked presumption in government contracts litigation that the contracting officer acted in good faith, making it easier for contractor to establish breach of contract by the government.

The Supreme Court has made plain time and again that when the government acts in its contractual, marketplace capacity-as opposed to its sovereign, regulatory capacity-the rules that control the government and those acting on its behalf are the same as those that apply to any two commercial contracting entities. Thus, in United States v. Winstar, 518 U.S. 839, 895 (1996), and again in Mobil Oil Exploration and

Producing Southeast, Inc. v. United States, 530 U.S. 604, 608 (2000), the Court expressly held that "[w]hen the United States enters into contract relations, its rights and duties therein are governed generally by the law applicable to contracts between private individuals."

Yet, for years the government has successfully defeated contractor claims for breach of contract by claiming that a contractor's allegations constitute, or amount to, claims that the contracting officer or other person acting on behalf of the government in administering a government contract acted in bad faith-and then claiming further that the contractor has failed to overcome the presumption that government actors perform their duties in good faith with "well-nigh irrefragable proof" to the contrary. The U.S. Court of Appeals for the Federal Circuit in Am-Pro Protective Agency, Inc. v. United States, 281 F.3d 1234 (Fed. Circ. 2002), equated this standard of proof to requiring "clear and convincing evidence." This high burden of proof, the government has successfully argued, requires a showing by the contractor that the government actor performed his or her duties with malice and a specific intent to injure the contractor.

In a spate of recent decisions by the U.S. Court of Federal Claims (COFC), this line of defense in government contracts litigation has been significantly eroded. Indeed, in H&S Manufacturing, Inc. v. United States, 66 Fed. Cl. 301 n.19 (July 18, 2005), the Court stated that the "Government's long touted desideratum that 'irrefragable proof' is needed to demonstrate the absence of good faith in the administration of government contracts has been given its last rites."

While some judges of the Court of Federal Claims have conferred "last rites" on the notion that "irrefragable proof' is needed to demonstrate the absence of good faith in the administration of government contracts," the question whether to resuscitate that principle ultimately is for the Federal Circuit to decide. Until then, however, the burden of the duty of good faith and fair dealing-including the duties to cooperate and not to interfere-has been relaxed considerably from that pressed by the government in recent years. (Scott McCaleb is a partner in the Washington, D.C., law firm of Wiley Rein & Fielding LLP.)

CHAPTER 3

Business Opportunity Development Reform Act of 1988
(Public Law 100-656)

124.1011   What is a misrepresentation of SBA STATUS?

a)   Any person or entity that misrepresents a firm's status as a "small business concern owned Socially
and economically disadvantaged individuals"
("SBA status") in order to obtain an 8(a) or SDB
contracting opportunity or preference will be subject to the penalties imposed by section 16 (d) of
the Small Business Act, 15 USC. 645 (d), as well
as any other penalty authorized law.

b)   A representation of SDB status by any firm that
SBA has found not to be an SDB (either in connection with an SDB application or protest) will be
deemed a misrepresentation of SDB status, unless

and until the firm reapplies for and obtains SDB certification.

Penalties-In addition to the penalties described in section 16 (d), any small business concern that is determined by the Administrator to have misrepresented the status of that concern as a small business concern owned and controlled by women for purposes of this subsection, shall be subject to

(i) Section 1001 of Title 18, United States Codes:

And

(ii) Section 3729 through 3733 of Title 31, United States Code.

Penalties:

The Business Opportunity Development Reform Act of 1988 (Public Law 100-656) provides for felony convictions up to 10 years, criminal fines of $500,000.00, mandatory 3 years debarments, and forfeitures for companies that are found to have misrepresented their small business status.

The amount of <u>fraud perpetrated against small and minority businesses is getting worse</u>, both in terms of the number of occurrences and the amount of money that is being lost. According to the American Small Business League and the US Congress, small businesses across the nation are losing contracts that were legally set aside for legitimate small businesses, due to large corporations fraudulently misrepresenting themselves as small businesses.

By failing to hold accountable these companies who misrepresent their business size, a message has been sent to the contracting community that there is no punishment for committing fraud. There is a need to put into place a mechanism to ensure that what happened to JCA will never again happen to another small business contractor. Small businesses can bring about change if they work together and force Congress--particularly the oversight committees--to investigate and compel the SBA to obey the law. While this requires work on the part of small businesses owners working together, it can be done.

CHAPTER 4

Government Accountability Office

"It is rare for a protester to win a protest, and even rarer for a winning protester to go on to obtain the contract at issue in the protest."

- Daniel I. Gordon

Government Accountability Office

Not too long ago I was again talking to my friend about the Trail of Tears. He was inquiring about how far along I was in writing my new book *The Great Wall of US*. I discussed where I was and started to talk about the government and how it seems that the way the government protects themselves is uncanny. In fact, it reminded me of the Great Wall of China. The method used to build the Great Wall of China is a series of fortifications made of stone, brick, wood, and other materials, generally built along an east-to-west line across the historical northern borders of China to protect the Chinese states and empires against the raids and invasions of the various nomadic groups.

As I see it, the US Court of Federal Claims and the GAO bid process are the Great Wall that protects the federal government. As I see it, the courts and government policies and regulations all are designed to protect the government from paying for its illegal activities. The regulations and policies are the bricks and wood, and other materials to protect the government.

As implied above, GAO is not the only forum with authority to hear bid protests involving federal acquisitions. The procuring agency and the US Court of Federal Claims can also hear bid protests. Federal agencies are required to award government contracts in accordance with numerous acquisition law and regulation, in a solicitation for goods or services, or in the award of a contract.

The US Court of Federal Claims and GAO, how these organizations operate and the similarity of their decisions can be important knowledge for a small contractor. If you are a small business with a government contract dispute and seek help from one of these organizations, you will not get the help you seek. These organizations are designed to protect the government and their respective agencies. In the case of GAO, if a company sustains a protest, there still isn't any guarantee that the contractor will keep the contract--in fact, in some cases, GAO never publishes its decisions.

According to a *New York Times* article dated December 27, 2006, titled "Small Business Fight Fickle Rules"….. "Many studies have shown that hundreds of government contracts set aside for small business are being awarded to large corporations. Federal laws provide several mechanisms that allow small-business owners who suspect that contracts have been awarded to large companies to protest.

"But small-business owners say that the rules in many cases impose nearly impossible standards on them. Even if they do succeed in protesting an award, they say, and prove that federal agencies are intentionally awarding small-business contracts to big companies, there are almost no penalties. Often, the large companies get to keep the contacts.

" 'It's a hollow victory,' said Raul Espinosa, a small-business owner in Florida who has won several protests. 'You might win the size protest, but you can't claim the contract because the agency allowed delivery to take place and what's worse, the penalties for the violations aren't enforced.'"

In 2014, GAO decided only 3.43% of protests cases

should be sustained (of 2,538 cases GAO sustained 87 cases) a very low number. This, however, is not the true story--the number is actually lower. For example, in many of the

protests presented before GAO, the procuring agency took some voluntary corrective action which granted some form of relief to the protester, which pre-empted GAO from rendering in a majority of the cases a protester- unfavorable decision.

Formal protests of US government contracts rarely help companies win a reversal of those awards, according to Daniel I. Gordon, President Obama's former procurement chief. In fiscal 2010, fewer than 15 protests filed with GAO resulted in the objecting party winning the work. That's less than 1 % of roughly 1,600 protested awards in that period, according to Dan Gordon. Looking at the US Court of Federal Claims cases on the docket during 2006, damages claims was in excess of $197 billion. The court rendered judgment in more than 900 cases and awarded $1.8 billion in damages--less than 1%.

Bid protesting can cost a great deal of money for a small business, and the government is aware of this fact. I was fortunate to have one of the best law firms in the country working for my firm pro bono. The firm was Howrey and Simon. I later found out that in man hours Howrey put in over $900,000 on my case over a 10-year period.

Fraud: Serious Business

The Government Accountability Office investigated an SBA-managed small business program and released Report 10-108, The Service-Disabled Veteran-Owned Small Business (SDVOSB), which essentially accused SBA executives of encouraging fraud. The report stated: "By failing to hold firms accountable, SBA and contracting agencies have sent a message to the contracting community that there is no punishment or consequences for committing fraud."

In the same report, GAO found the SBA does not have "effective fraud-prevention controls in place." Fraud and abuse in the SDVOSB program allowed ineligible firms to improperly receive millions of dollars in set-aside and sole-source SDVOSB contracts, potentially denying legitimate service-disabled veterans and their firms the benefits of this program. We identified 10 case-study examples of firms that did not meet SDVOSB program eligibility requirements, received approximately $100 million in SDVOSB contracts, and over $300 million in additional dollars of 8(a), HUBZone.

In GAO-10-424, report to the US House Committee on Small Business, identifies $325 million in set aside and sole-source contracts given to firms not eligible for the 8(a) program. Most were obtained through fraudulent schemes. In the 14 cases GAO investigated, numerous instances were found where unqualified 8(a) firm presidents made false statements, such as underreporting income or assets, to either quality for the program or retain certification. "In some cases, SBA did not detect the false statements and misrepresentations made by certified firms. In others, SBA became aware of the firms' ineligibility but failed to take action."

In this same GAO report, it states SBA is providing inaccurate or in complete information to the Congress and general public on SBA contracting activities. Clearly, SBA has been and is intentionally falsifying the volume and %age of federal contracts awarded to small businesses. Not only is this behavior deplorable, but it is wrong for a government agency to act in this manner. Given all of the above, it is curious that the Justice Department OIG or SBA OIG has not taken any action to correct the problems.

CHAPTER 5

Government Fraud SBA Problem

"How Small-Business Issues Are Shaping Politics and Policy" - *NY Times* 11/01/11

The New York Times

You're the Boss

Fraud and Loopholes Deliver Small-Business Contracts to Big Firms

By Robb Mandelbaum

November 1, 2011 2:00 pm

The Agenda

How small-business issues are shaping politics and policy.

It's been a busy season for combating fraud in government contracts for small business, for prosecutors enforcing the law as well as the legislators trying to improve it. But for both, it appears to be an uphill battle.

In June, the federal government charged two men with creating a fake small business to win a $100 million Defense Department contract. Two months later, a businessman pleaded guilty to obtaining a false citizenship papers, which he used to get a security clearance from the Department of Defense so that he could receive preferential small-business contracts.

In October, one man pleaded guilty to a scheme in which he and a partner vouched for the small-business status of each other's company. That, in turn, led the Justice Department to uncover an alleged ring of bribery and kickbacks centered at Eyak Technology, or EyakTek, nominally a small business based in Virginia with a $1 billion contract to provide information and security technology to government agencies. An indictment announced on Oct. 4 claims that the company's contracting director conspired with officials in the Army Corps of Engineers to steer federal purchases to an unnamed subcontractor. That subcontractor then inflated its bills by $20 million, according to the indictment and used part of the proceeds to pay off the Eyak and Army Corps officials.

The federal government is the world's largest buyer

of goods and service, and it is supposed to make sure that 23 % of those purchases go to small businesses. In the case of economically disadvantaged business-es, government agencies can often set aside contracts and award them without putting them up for a com-petitive bid. The government perennially misses those goals, but most observers believe that the amount of small-business contracts the government does report masks a share that have in fact been diverted to larger companies. Fraud is an important, though unquanti-fied, culprit.

Observers say government officials in charge of procurement are often too busy to look closely at a company's small-business credentials. But the Small Business Administration's inspector general, Peggy E. Gustafson, testifying in a Congressional hearing last week, said that her agency often did not effectively oversee the contracting programs and did not aggres-sively pursue companies that misrepresented them-selves as small. The SBA, Ms. Gustafson said in her prepared statement, "needs to change its culture so that employees understand that their mission includes not only assisting small businesses but also ensuring accountability and integrity to prevent fraudulent and improper actions from depriving procurement oppor-tunities for legitimate firms."

Ms. Gustafson also said that despite the recent le-gal victories, seeking justice in a courtroom was dif-ficult because a company that fraudulently identifies itself as small in order to win a federal contract usually fulfills the contract. "Without an associated and definable loss to the government, criminal prosecutors are sometimes reluctant to pursue action against these companies, or if they do pursue them, may only be able to obtain limited sentences," she said.

That is not the case in the EyakTek case, where the government allegedly paid for the conspirators' BMWs, first-class airfares and Cartier watches. But while the company itself was not implicated in wrongdoing-charges were only brought against its head of contracting-the allegations surrounding EyakTek raised other troubling questions about small-business contracting, because the company had a legally sanctioned leg up in the competition for small-business contracts. Eyak is what's known as an Alaska Native Corporation, and with that designation, it is able to complete for contracts set aside for companies that participate in the SBA's 8(a) program. This is a program intended to help small, disadvantaged businesses-particularly those owned by minorities-by providing business training coupled with opportunities for no-bid contracts set aside just for them.

In the 1970s Congress made Alaska Native Corporations a special class of 8(a) business. Unlike most businesses in the program, the Alaskan companies are not subject to a limit to the size of a no-bid contract. And while a typical 8(a) business must be managed by someone who meets the program's definition of disadvantaged, that's not the case with Alaska Native Corporations, which tend to recruit executives with broad and deep ties across government agencies and pay handsomely for their experience.

These features have made Alaska Native Corporations very popular with government bureaucrats because they offer an easy way to meet small-business quotas. In 2009, according to the SBA's inspector general, Alaskan firms took in 26 % of total 8(a) contract dollars. EyakTek and other subsidiaries of the Eyak Corporation together took in a least $338 Million, according to a search of the federal contracting records performed by the American Small Business League, which lobbies for integrity in small-business contracting. (If a native company gets too big to participate in the program, the parent corporation can simply create a new company-another advantage not afforded other program participants.)

Any effort to change the rules for Alaskan companies is likely to meet stiff resistance in Congress. (Alaska's representative, Don Young, is the second-ranked Republican in the House in terms of seniority and the sixth most senior of all representatives.)

Surprisingly, even trying to pass legislation to curb fraud is more difficult than one might expect. In her testimony, Ms. Gustafson proposed measures to make it easier to prosecute fraud and stiffen penalties for conviction, in part by defining a loss to the government as equal to the size of the contract.

A bill containing these provisions has passed the Senate, but Rep. Sam Graves, the Chairman of the House Small Business Committee, faulted the Senate bill for, among other things, not including an exemption for honest errors. "The small business affiliation rules are complex and are not intuitive, so I'm hesitant to potentially trigger jail time for companies that make a mistake," he said in an interview with VetLikeMe, a newsletter for business owners who are wounded veterans, "although I agree that we need to more vigorously enforce the certification rules." The House has not yet taken up the Senate bill.

Mr. Graves also expressed skepticism about a separate House bill, introduced last month that would exclude the subsidiaries of publicly traded companies from the definition of a small-business contractor. The law already requires that recipients of small-business contracts must be independently owned and operated, but an American Small Business League spokesman, Brian Reeder, said a clarification was necessary. "Common sense says that independently owned means not publicly traded," he said, "yet publicly traded companies and their subsidiaries receive contracts that government agencies put toward their small business goals."

The bill was introduced by Rep. Hank Johnson, a Georgia Democrat, with support from 16 other Democrats. No Republicans sponsored the legislation, and Mr. Graves, the Small Business Committee chairman, opposes the bill "because it places further restrictions on how a small business can be organized and the source of its investment," said a spokesman, Darrell Jordan. "At a time of record unemployment, Chairman Graves wants to support measures that help small businesses grow."

Opposition to Mr. Johnson's measure isn't strictly partisan. The Georgia congressman introduced an identical bill last year, while Democrats were in charge. It died in committee.

SBA Problem / Issues Fraud

A troublesome problem facing small businesses in dealing with federal government contract programs is fraud, abuse, and loopholes in federal policies, allowing the majority of federal small business contracts to be illegally diverted to large corporations. Over the years, SBA has used numerous reasons as to why large contractors received hundreds of billions of dollars in federal small business contracts, including miscoding, simple human error, and mistakes. In an investigative report by CBS, the SBA claimed 235 Fortune 500 firms had received billions in federal small business contracts accidentally through "simple human error." They were unable to explain why the alleged errors always diverted small business contracts to Fortune 500 firms.

While a majority of Americans said the Cherokee are "savage," many government contracting officers say small businesses can't do the big contract work; therefore, they are not entitled to big contract awards. The arguments used by the government 200 years ago are the same as today in that they play to people's fears and prejudices. In the case of the Cherokee, it was the fact that they were Indians. They supposedly had too much land and they would raid European settlers and kill them in their sleep. In the case of the small business, supposedly they are unprepared to deal with the laws and regulations that are unique to the government. Being unprepared, many small businesses find themselves caught up in costly errors and potential negative legal problems.

In 2012, General Dynamics, with 81,000 employees and more than $21 billion in annual revenue, received at least $215 million in small business contracts. At the same time, Italian conglomerate Finmeccanica received over $5.1 million in US small business contracts. The SBA inspector general has named the diversion of federal small business contracts as the number-one challenge at the SBA for the last nine consecutive years. However, neither SBA nor the Justice Department has done anything to correct this illegal problem. Every small business should have a how to protect your business against government contract fraud policy. There isn't any question that fraud impacts a small business bottom-line. Therefore, it is important that small businesses develop policies that address this issue. The best way to understand how to protect your business is to get a good lawyer who is knowledgeable about small business law--this is the key for any small business.

SBA has the responsibility to protect small businesses and to make sure that the laws and regulations impacting small business are enforced. Congress gave this authority to SBA over 50 years ago. For many years, I have wondered why SBA ignored the law and regulations involving small business set-aside contracts going to small businesses--was it due to incompetence, or was it calculated? I believe it's a little of both, with heavy emphasis on calculated. SBA has the legal authority to compel the contracting agencies to fulfill their proper obligations to SBA and small-business contractors. In JCA case, the INS a federal executive agency, engaged in patently unscrupulous conduct under its contract with JCA. Small businesses should be aware that Congress has the power to provide "equitable" relief to contractors who have clearly been wronged but have no legal remedy. It is not easy to get a Congressional representative to act in this area; however, it is possible.

CHAPTER 6

Using Fraud in the SBA 8(a) Program Is Not New to SBA

President Richard Nixon (1969–74) boosted the SBA's minority enterprise programs by advocating "black capitalism," a term that embraced nonwhite minorities, including African-Americans, Hispanics, Native Americans, and Asian-Americans. The SBA used its authority under Section 8(a) of the Small Business Act to set aside no-bid contracts for "socially and economically disadvantaged" business owners, a euphemism for minorities. Section 8(a) set-asides were enormously controversial, as critics charged "reverse discrimination" against white business owners. The SBA has the power to set aside government contracts for small firms, thus excluding larger businesses from competing. Set-aside contracts are negotiated (given to an individual firm) or opened to bidding by small businesses. They make up half of all government contracts awarded to small firms.

Since the 1970s, periodic scandals have erupted as journalists and prosecutors uncovered widespread corruption, particularly the fraudulent use of minority "fronts" by white business owners. Two scandals involving SBA minority enterprise programs—Wed Tech and Whitewater—embarrassed the presidential administrations of Ronald Reagan and William Clinton, respectively. Nevertheless, Section 8(a) has withstood court challenges. Moreover, 8(a) group eligibility criteria, first developed in 1980, have become the standard for other agencies' affirmative action programs.

Fraud - Small Business and JCA

I was surprised to learn that if the government participates in or is aware of a crime being committed, then it is not a crime, and the government cannot be held accountable. That is what happened in my case. US District Court for the District of Columbia United States of America, ex rel. J. Cooper & Associates, Inc. Plaintiff v. Bernard Hodes Group, Inc., CASS

Communications, Inc., and J. Walter Thompson Co. Defendants (Civil Action No.:03-2436 (RMU).

The court ruled, *"The government's decision to award contracts to the defendants, despite its knowledge that the defendants were not small or disadvantaged businesses, negates any claim of fraud against the defendants."* A couple of things stand out in Judge Urbina's decisions that are worth mentioning.

First, District Judge Ricardo M. Urbina acknowledged in his decision that the defendants, J. Walter Thompson, Bernard Hodes Group, and CASS Communications, did misrepresent themselves as "disadvantaged" businesses, when, in fact, they were not. He ruled that *"The evidence in this case shows that the INS was aware that the defendants were not small and or disadvantaged businesses and offered them advertising and public relations contracts anyway."*

Second, the court stated that numerous media reports on the defendants would suffice to *"set government investigators on the trail of fraud,"* and

Third, the court stated, *"During the course of the plaintiff's suit against the government. However, the INS explicitly admitted that it "obtained with the concurrence of SBA, some advertising services from other vendors outside the section 8(a) program" and even named defendant JWT as one such vendor."*

The INS never obtained SBA's "concurrence" to use non-Section 8(a) contractors to implement the INS requirement. On May 16, 1996, the INS letter to the SBA was the first time the INS notified the SBA that it planned to use non-Section 8(a) contractors for the INS requirement. The INS had been using non-Section 8(a) contractors who were claiming to be disadvantaged businesses for months prior to the May 16, 1996 letter. The INS could never produce any written documents from the SBA authorizing the INS to use non-Section 8(a) contractors to implement its requirement. Verbal authorization is not sufficient for such a modification of a SBA 8(a) set-aside contract. FAR regulations and SBA policies require written authorization from the SBA to the INS to implement such modifications. This never occurred.

Even though the court ruled that the contractors did not commit fraud under the False Claims Act, the Business Opportunity Development Reform Act of 1988 (P.L. 100-656) had been violated, along with numerous FAR Regulations. The court made no mention of these violations. The court did suggest that the government investigators should explore fraud. However, given this decision, neither the SBA IG nor DOJ IG took any action to resolve this issue.

The one law or legislation that all lawful government authorities, SBA IG, DOJ IG and the courts should be concerned with when the issue of federal government contract fraud comes up is the Business Opportunity Development Reform Act of 1988 (P.L. 100-656). This legislation addresses the heart of all small-business contracts that are set aside, that are fraudulently given to big businesses. It states that it is illegal for companies to misrepresent their business status in order to acquire set-aside small-business government contracts. If caught, this crime is punishable by fine and or prison term, yet not one corporation has ever been prosecuted for misrepresenting itself as a small or disadvantaged business by the SBA.

Like the Cherokee Indians 200 years ago, when they won their court victory, President Andrew Jackson stated he would do nothing to enforce the law or help the Cherokee. In JCA's case, the government failed to enforce the law by implementing the Business Opportunity Reform Act of 1988 (P.L. 100-656). They also failed to enforce the FAR's and SBA's numerous policies related to their set-aside program. Like the Cherokee, I pleaded with the government and Congress for assistance, to no avail.

SBA Falling Short of Meeting Its Contract Goals to Small business

SBA ᎡᎤᎦᏐ ᏅᎤᏯᎯᏈᏀᏐᎥᎤᏭ-ᏅᎯᎰᏈᏎᏛᎤᎤᎴ ᏞᏞᏁᏘᏴᎯ ᏥᎾᎤᎥᏛ ᏅᏍᏛᏎᏭᎳᎤᎤ ᎨᎤᎩᏛ ᏧᎤᏛᏞ ᏤᏍᎯᏎᎤᏛᏞᏁᏞ SVPRT ᏤᎤᏐᏊᏛᏐ

The issue of how the federal government spends the contract money it sets aside for small businesses is critical not only to small businesses, but also to the communities in which those small businesses are located. Often, those communities have many small businesses with fewer than twenty employees. These small businesses can be the lifeblood of the communities and their economy. It is important that small businesses get the contracts that are set aside for them.

In 2014 the US government will again fall short of its small-business contracting goal. Despite all the expansion of the small-business market this year, the government still has not reached its goal to award contracts to small businesses. According to the Small Business Administration, the federal government is falling short of its goals for awarding contracts to small businesses in some industries where it spends the most money. Small businesses should never lose sight of the fact that the government has an overall goal of giving 23 % of its contracting dollars to small businesses. This is the law.

According to the SBA Office of Advocacy, small

businesses make up more than 56 % of the US economy, provide 75 % of the net new jobs added to the economy, represent 99.7 % of all employers, employ 50.7 % of the private workforce, provide 40.9 % of private sales in the country, and represent 97 % of all US exporters. This is even despite the billions each year in federal "small business" contracts that are instead given to large and international corporations being counted toward the federal small business procurement goal.

Many government investigations and private studies conducted since 2003 have verified that hundreds of government contracts set aside for small businesses have instead been awarded to Fortune 500 corporations claiming to be small businesses. They are awarded over $135 billion a year. As far back as I can remember, the SBA has attempted to justify the diversion of billions in small business contracts to Fortune 500 firms as "miscoding." In 2006 the SBA issued a press release, claiming the diversion of federal small business contracts to large firms was a "myth." During this same period, Karen Hontz, the SBA's associate administrator for government contracting, stated, "We're looking into...miscoding discrepancies. We will have an explanation, but it takes time." Five years later, the fraudulent activities committed by large government contractors are still going on.

The SBA inspector general has named the diversion of federal small business contracts as the number-one challenge at the SBA for the last nine consecutive years. However, neither SBA nor the Justice Department has done anything to correct this illegal problem. Every small business should have a how to protect your business against government contract fraud policy. There isn't any question that fraud impacts a small business' bottom line; therefore, it is important that small businesses develop policies that address this issue. Small businesses across the nation are losing contracts due to large corporations fraudulently misrepresenting themselves as small businesses.

CHAPTER 7

J. Cooper & Associates, Inc.

If you are a small-business owner, you can remember how scary it was before you started your business. You were scared, but you saw others do it, so you knew that you could do it too. You had the confidence and the desire to share in the American dream--it was a tremendous enticement. You made a commitment to yourself that you would work hard, put in long hours, and do whatever it takes to be successful, because you left the security of the corporate life or steady job behind. You wanted to make life better for yourself and your family.

Then you hear that the federal government is keeping you from receiving federal government contracts that Congress requires to be set aside (small business set-aside is a powerful tool to help small business win prime contracts) for you, because your company is a small business. You hear that it involves contracts worth thousands, hundreds of thousands of dollars. You think to yourself that this is a great opportunity when you discover that the government is working at giving the contracts to big corporations who are committing fraud by claiming to be small businesses in order to qualify for receiving these contracts. To make matters shameless, the SBA, courts, and Congress are aware of what is going on and nobody is doing anything to correct the problem.

In July 1995, the Immigration and Naturalization Service (INS) awarded an $8-million-dollar contract to J. Cooper and Associates (JCA) to provide advertising services for the SBA Section 8(a) set-aside program for small, disadvantaged businesses. By using the section 8(a) set-aside program, it allowed the award to take place faster for the government. The INS stopped issuing orders for services to JCA six months into the contract. An INS official responsible for the advertising program decided to issue orders to companies with which she had previously worked. Those companies were large advertising entities-- clearly not Section 8(a) companies. The fact was presented in court and confirmed by the INS Office of the Inspector General. The organizations profiting from the action of the INS employee included the J. Walter Thompson Company, the Bernard Hodes Group, and Cass Communications.

These organizations denied participation in any fraudulent action. The organizations stated that they did not commit fraud, since the INS knew the true status when the work was awarded. Bruce M. Ginsberg, (JWT lawyer) of the law firm of Davis and Gilbert, representing the organizations in court, stated that the multi-million dollar companies "would not represent themselves as small businesses. We have no idea how they came to be marked that way in the INS documents." However, JWT failed to act ethically by reminding the INS that they could not accept the contract because of their non-status as small or disadvantaged.

Experience points to the fact that this was not an unusual situation. Studies showed that hundreds of government contracts set aside for small businesses were awarded to large corporations and still are to this day. Although mechanisms exist to allow small-business owners to challenge contract awards such as this, the rules impose impossible standards of proof on them. Additionally, if they are successful, there are no penalties for the large companies who get to keep the contracts making any winning court action by the 8(a) set-aside business a hollow victory.

Today when a small business files a complaint or protest against a set-aside contract that has been awarded to a big company, the small business is frequently told that the contract was not a set-side, thus no grounds for a protest. For the last several years the SBA has dismissed hundreds of legitimate protests from small businesses, claiming that the contract was not a set-aside.

Recently, it has become difficult to bring an action against a big company for contract fraud unless it can be shown that the large contractor intended to commit fraud. Needless to say, this is hard to accomplish. It does show the limits our government will go to protect the status quo.

Small Business Owners, should get together with each other to talk about changing the system. If meetings can't take place in person than use of the internet would do well.

The strength of JCA case centers around the revelations that the INS program staff and contracting officials both knew or had reason to know that JCA's competitors had falsely certified themselves as small, disadvantaged businesses, but the officials repeatedly contracted with those competitors, to JCA's detriment.

Government contracting can be a wonderful source of revenue for small business in the area of growth. It is absolutely vital for small businesses looking forward to getting into the federal government market take advantage of all the opportunities available to them to market their capabilities to contracting officers. As a small business owner, it's important that you not be naïve about business practices, or you'll go broke. That is why it is important that you fight for your piece of the pie. Set-aside contracts were set up to help small businesses grow their business.

Understanding Your Contract

When I realized that my contract with INS would be an IDIQ contract, I knew I was in trouble. I hate IDIQ contracts because they are designed to totally protect the government, with little consideration for the small contractor. For example: Some IDIQ contracts require a sizeable investment to compete for an award. The government may not fund and award an IDIQ in a timely manner. One of the major troubling problems I have is that even if you win an IDIQ contract, you may be awarded very little task or work and revenue. Depending upon the contract and the task orders, you may receive few fees and no profit.

Years ago when I first learned about IDIQ contracts, I thought it would afford my company the opportunity to grow and compete for lots of work and make good revenue. I was looking forward to working with subcontractors to expand work and develop business relationships with government and other contractors.

I made several mistakes in my dispute with the INS and the SBA. The government wanted to control my contract and business, and I allowed it to happen. I diverted my attention from my private-sector business to deal with the government problems instead of continuing to give more attention to building up my private-sector business.

Background J. Cooper and Associates, Inc.

ᏍᏳᎫᏢ ᏈᏬᏍᏐ J. Cooper ᎠᏍ ᏓᎠᎠᎢᎠᏍᎱᎧ ᏌᏎᏨᎭᏍᎢ.

Joseph N. Cooper founded JCA in 1987 upon his departure from the federal government, where he had served as the director of the Office of Federal Contract Compliance Programs ("OFCCP") from 1985 to 1987. As a former director of the OFCCP, Mr. Cooper was well known to the government contracting community and enjoyed an excellent reputation in that community.

As president of JCA, Mr. Cooper operated the company as a minority-owned small business that provided a variety of consulting services, including public relations and advertising services. JCA's clients included Fortune 500 corporations such as Aetna Insurance,

United Technologies, MCI, McDonnell Douglas, and Colgate Palmolive, as well as state governments and federal agencies. In 1992, JCA applied to the SBA to obtain certification to participate in the SBA Section 8(a) Program. In 1994, JCA had qualified for 8(a) certification. Also in 1994, JCA received the SBA's Minority Service Firm of the Year award. From its inception until it began performing under a letter contract with the INS, JCA had consistently earned a profit and maintained an excellent business reputation.

In early 1995, JCA, SBA, and INS started pre-contract discussions and the Award of the Letter Contract. The INS began efforts to select a contractor to perform an urgent INS requirement ("the requirement") for advertising and public relations services. The requirement involved the development and implementation of a marketing and advertising plan to improve and increase the recruitment of candidates for the Border Patrol and other offices of the INS. INS officials explored several options by which the requirement could be placed under contract as quickly as possible, including, inter alia, opening the procurement to full competition or limiting the procurement to the SBA 8(a) Program for Small and Disadvantaged Businesses ("SDB"). The INS acknowledged that one of the principal advantages offered by contracting with the Section 8(a) program was that a contract for the requirement could be awarded as early as July 1995, whereas if the requirement were opened to full competition, the contract could not be awarded until sometime in September 1995.

In or around mid-May 1995, the SBA Business Opportunity Specialist ("BOS") identified JCA as an 8(a) program SDB that possessed the qualifications to satisfy the requirement; and in June 1995, INS officials held meetings with JCA representatives regarding the requirement. During those June 1995 meetings, INS officials informed JCA that (1) the requirement would involve a number of varied and discrete tasks, such as placing advertisements in selected print and electronic media, preparing video tape presentations, and preparing a strategic plan to address the overall public relations and recruitment campaign; and (2) INS officials did not intend to contract separately with different contractors for each of the discrete tasks under the Contract but, instead, intended to have all of the public relations and advertising services performed by one contractor.

During the June 1995 meetings, INS officials informed JCA that the requirement would involve a possible multiyear, multimillion-dollar effort and stressed the urgency of the requirement. INS officials also informed JCA that it would need to have sufficient personnel and resources to handle a significant amount of immediate tasking from the INS and that

JCA would need to hire additional personnel and to obtain facilities to ensure prompt performance of the anticipated tasks.

Also during the June 1995 meetings, INS officials informed JCA that the INS intended to award the contract for the requirement to JCA. At no time during any of the June 1995 meetings with JCA did the INS ever inform or indicate to JCA that the INS intended to use any contractor other than JCA to perform the INS requirement while JCA performed under the letter contract.

On June 30, 1995, the INS prepared a determination and findings memorandum, stating that the INS intended to process the requirement through the SBA as "an 8(a) requirement" and that the INS intended to enter into a letter contract to give JCA a binding commitment to begin work immediately on the INS requirement. JCA was the sole contractor for which the INS sought authorization to enter into a letter contract for the requirement. On July 7, 1995, the INS sent an "offering letter" to the SBA to offer the INS requirement to the Section 8(a) program. The offering letter estimated that the requirement would be valued at approximately $8 million over a five-year period. On or about July 7, 1995, the SBA accepted the entire INS requirement as a "set-aside" requirement for both the SBA 8(a) program and JCA.

The Harris Bank / DCAA Audit

Toward the end of October 1995, JCA became concerned about its difficulties both with receiving
payment from the INS and with satisfying the requests
of the Defense Contract Auditing Agency ("DCAA")
auditor who had been assigned to review JCA's proposal for the definitization of the contract.

Beginning in early October 1995, JCA began sending
the SBA BOS a series of courtesy copies of the corre-
spondence that JCA was sending to the INS and to the
DCAA regarding the problems that JCA was having
with both receiving payment and the audit issues on
the contract. The SBA failed to respond to any of this
correspondence with any guidance or assistance until January 1996. In fact, JCA received no response of
guidance and assistance from the SBA until sometime
in January 1996—more than three months after JCA
first requested assistance.

During the DCAA audit I was told by the auditor that
my presence would be necessary while the auditor was
on premises conducting her review. This presented a
problem for me because it prevented me from visiting
my private-sector clients. Actually, there wasn't any
need for me to be at the audit, because I had my ac-
countants present working with the auditor. When I
objected to being present, the auditor informed me
that she would have to stop the audit. I had planned

a meeting in Chicago at Harris Bank to meet with senior staff to discuss some pressing personnel problems they were having. I felt the squeeze in that the INS had requested the audit, and my private client needed me to discuss pressing matters.

Here is where I made a big mistake. I put the government business first because I wanted to keep the $8 million INS contract. In addition, I was on the verge of getting a $5 million contract from the Defense Department to help handle a piece of the Army recruiting campaign. This contract had not been confirmed, but we had just scheduled to work out the details. JCA was getting this contract because it was an SBA 8(a) setaside contactor and the only qualified contractor in the area at the time who could provide the full service needed. Needless to say, when word got out concerning the problems my business was having with the INS, this opportunity went south and SBA did nothing to help JCA.

The long and short of it is that I did not show in Chicago, sending instead Gil, my associate, in my place. This did not go over well with the executives at the bank. The next day I received a call from Trevor, who informed me that JCA's services would no longer be needed. At the time, I felt bad--not because I just lost a major piece of business, but I lost good friends, people I had enjoyed working with over the years.

My experience with the government is not about me anymore; it's about my wanting to help other small business owners avoid going through the years of pain and suffering I went through. I want my story to be a wake-up call to small business owners to be aware of the government contract program and frankly run for your life when it comes to dealing with federal government contracts. I want it to be clear how the federal government just takes illegally what's not theirs to take--the unfairness, hypocrisy, the graft, and the devastating results.

SBA's Failure to Respond to JCA's Multiple Pleas for Assistance

JCA's ᎣᎪᏢ ᎢᎬᏀᎳ ᏞᏫᎡᎭᏉᎤ ᎠᏢᎤᎦᏒᎭᏞ ᎤᏉᎠᎩ SBA Ꮈ ᏣᏃᏢᏴᎤᎳᏁᎢ

From the award of the contract until late September 1995, JCA performed oral task orders as directed by INS personnel, and during this period JCA received only positive feedback on its performance under the contract. Toward the end of October 1995, however, JCA became concerned about its difficulties both with receiving payment from the INS and with satisfying the requests of the Defense Contract Auditing Agency ("DCAA") auditor who had been assigned to review JCA's proposal for the definitization of the contract.

In late September, JCA telephoned SBA officials to obtain guidance and assistance regarding the difficulties that JCA was having with the INS and the DCAA. However, no one from the SBA returned JCA's calls with any guidance or assistance. Next, on October 20, 1995, JCA sent a letter to the SBA BOS, in which JCA requested the SBA's assistance with the difficulties that JCA was experiencing under the contract. JCA informed the SBA BOS that

(a) The INS's failure to issue task orders to JCA had presented a "serious financial problem" for JCA;

(b) JCA had "geared up" for the contract by hiring additional personnel, buying additional equipment, obtaining additional office space, expanding its phone system, recruiting additional staff, and establishing an employee benefits plan, and because JCA did not have tasks to implement, JCA was "at risk financially";

(c) JCA had had trouble collecting payment for services rendered and that one invoice was already ninety days in arrears; and

(d) JCA, "as a small business... [could not] withstand the level of delinquency that INS ha[d] imposed though failure to process invoices in a timely manner, or failure to release tasks in sufficient quantity to allow JCA to be success-ful." In the same letter, JCA also requested the SBA's assistance in arranging a tripartite meet-ing among JCA, SBA, and the INS to address the issues that had arisen under the contract.

The SBA did not respond to the JCA's "October 20, 1995 letter" with any guidance or assistance until January 1996.

Beginning in early October 1995, JCA began sending the SBA BOS a series of courtesy copies of the corre-spondence that JCA was sending to the INS and to the DCAA regarding the problems that JCA was having with both receiving payment and the audit issues on the contract. The SBA failed to respond to any of this correspondence with any guidance or assistance un-til January 1996. In fact, JCA received no response of guidance and assistance from the SBA until sometime in January 1996—more than three months after JCA first requested assistance.

I spent a lot of time writing to Congresswoman Nydia M. Velazquez, D-NY, and former chairwoman of the House Small Business Committee. She stated in an NY Times article dated December 27, 2006, that she would "work to rectify the problems faced by Mr.

Cooper and other small businesses by ensuring that there is an effective protest system in place." She also stated that she wanted "to make sure that penalties are in place." On August 16, 2006, she stated, "What we are seeing is a sheer lack of accountability from the administration that is resulting in these large businesses receiving Small Business Awards." She further stated, "As a consequence, entrepreneurs are getting less and less contracting opportunities each year." It's ironic, but the same problems still exist today.

No matter how one evaluates the facts and evidence of this case, J. Walter Thompson, Bernard Hodes, and Cass Communications lied on government orders, representing themselves as disadvantaged businesses when, in fact, they were not. They took this action with the INS's cooperation to acquire the government contract set aside for JCA as an SBA 8(a) contractor. Laws were broken, and JCA went out of business.

SBA's only concern should have been to protect its 8(a) contractor and see that it was treated fairly by the INS. Instead, SBA was more concerned with protecting special-interest group companies J. Walter Thompson, Bernard Hodes, and CASS Communications. To accomplish this objective, SBA lied, misrepresented the truth, and failed to enforce the law. There was no accountability to ensure that the SBA followed the law and did its job. SBA clearly writes its own laws and ignores Congressional laws as it sees fit. Needless to say, this behavior was very similar to how Andrew Jackson dealt with the Cherokee Indians.

CHAPTER 8

Small Business Trail of Tears

The Education Begins

In 1830, Congress passed the Indian Removal Act, which gave the federal government all the power needed to relocate all Native Americans in the southeastern part of the United States to the Indian Territory in Oklahoma. President Andrew Jackson was a strong supporter of this legislation. He had urged Congress to pass it. Actually, it was President James Monroe, in his final address to the Congress in 1825, who recommended to Jackson that he support the Indian Removal Act. This bill was Jackson's way to gain control over all Indian land, particularly the Cherokee. Native Americans were to be compensated. However, this was not always done impartially.

The Cherokee was allocated land in Georgia as a result of the 1791 treaty with the US Government. In

1828, not only did the Europeans—or Euros, for set-tlement purposes--desire Cherokee land, but gold was discovered in Georgia in 1829. At this point, Euro set-tlers' desires for Indian land were in a frenzy, and the settlers would do anything to get the land, including killing women and children.

Georgia tried to reclaim this land in 1830, but the Cherokee protested and took their case to the US Supreme Court. The court decided in favor of the Cherokee. The decision upset President Andrew Jackson, to the point of his refusal to enforce the deci-sion. Nevertheless, the president and Congress forced the Natives to give up their land.

At the beginning of the 1830s, nearly 125,000 Native Americans lived on millions of acres of land in Georgia, Tennessee, Alabama, North Carolina, and Florida–land their ancestors had occupied and cultivated for generations. By the end of the decade, very few Natives remained anywhere in the south-eastern United States. Working on behalf of the Euro settlers who wanted to grow cotton on the Indians' land, the federal government forced them to leave their homelands and walk thousands of miles to a specially designated "Indian territory" west across the Mississippi River. This difficult and sometimes deadly journey is known as "The Trail Where They Cried," or better known as the "Trail of Tears."

In order to understand why there were little opposition to the Indian Removal Act, to clear the land for white occupancy between the Appalachians and Mississippi--important for the growth of cotton, immigration expansion, new cities, and railroad that would lead to the great Pacific--you need to understand the war of 1812 between America and Great Britain and what took place in America after the war ended.

Many Americans don't understand or know for that matter that during the Revolutionary War over 90% of every important Indian Nation in America fought alongside the British. Once they signed for peace and the war ended, the British went back to England and the Indians stayed in America, losing every day. Statistics are clear. In 1790 3.9 million Americans lived in the United States. The majority lived within 50 miles of the Atlantic Ocean. The majority of Indians lived east of the Mississippi; they were fighting and trying to get along with a recent enemy, and it was not working out. Most of these Indians had been forced to migrate westward. Whites were increasing in number and land was needed desperately for farmers and the new settlers. The only land available was Indian land—the land of a defeated enemy. The problem for the white settlers was that the Indian land had treaties which the government was to adhere to.

Secretary of war Henry Knox said, the Indians being

the prior occupants possessed the right of the soil. Secretary of State Thomas Jefferson, said in 1791, where Indians lived within state boundaries they should not be interfered with, and that the government should remove white settlers who tried to encroach on them.

One could say this was the time and beginning of the government's efforts to steal and take Indian land for their own purpose. The US government had a need to make land available to new settlers and farmers--13 million Americans and growing. By 1840 4.5 million had crossed into the Mississippi Valley and crossed over the Appalachian mountains. It is clear that during this period in American history Indian removal was necessary in order to make way for new settlers and farmers. The difficulty centered on how the government would acquire this land legally without taking or stealing from the Indians. America was coming into its own toward becoming an economic power. This meant vast amount of land open to agriculture, to commerce, markets, and developing money to open new markets.

John Donaldson, a surveyor, owned over 20,000 acres of land near what is now Chattanooga. After the Revolution, large chunks of Chickasaw land was purchased by rich speculators, farmers, and settlers. Donaldson--the father-in-law of Andrew Jackson, who later became president of the United States--was a slave trader, and merchant. Most important of all Jackson, was the biggest and baddest enemy of the Native Americans in early American history. Jackson was a hero of the War of 1812 against England for survival. It was not a war for survival--it was a war to help a young country grow by acquiring land for expansion in a new country into Florida and Indian Territory.

Aside from buying all the land they could from the Chickasaw, Jackson and his friends got Jackson appointed treaty commissioner. He dictated a treaty that took half of the Creek nation's land away from them. This land treaty goes down in American history as one of the biggest Indian secessions of Southern American land. This was the beginning of stealing Native American land and doing whatever was necessary to remove Indians from their land. I am not sure Jackson at the time realize that the treaties and land grabs laid the foundation for the cotton empires and slave plantations. Each time that treaties were signed, requiring the Creeks to be pushed off their land to the next, they were promised that this would be the last time, they were told whites would not move on this property. At this point Jackson had brought the white settlers to the border of Florida, which at this time was owned by Spain.

This is where the Seminole Indians came into play.

Jackson had brought white settlers at the doorsteps of the Seminole villages. Here again Jackson made the white settlers take Seminole land. British agents and Seminole opposed the action of the US government and there were many Seminole who refused to leave. The Seminole were accused of murdering whites, and Jackson ordered many Seminole villages destroyed. This was the beginning of the Seminole War of 1818, which led to the acquisition of Florida as a direct result of Andrew Jackson's military campaign across the Florida border, destroying and burning Seminole villages, capturing Spanish forts, forcing Spain to sell Florida. Jackson is quoted as saying he acted by the "immutable" laws of self-defense. The Seminole fought the US government to the point that the government paid the Seminole a reported large sum to go west, which many did.

It's worth mentioning that the term "Trail of Tears" was first used in 1831 with the removal of the Choctaw, the first tribe to move west of the Mississippi. Not until the removal of the Cherokee did the term stick. The government started moving 15,000 Cherokee in 1838: men, women, and children not counting the old, sick, and some slaves the Cherokee owned. The march was over 1000 miles toward Oklahoma, the Indian Territory. The marching conditions were horrible for the people. Health conditions were poor--people had little food. Many had little clothing and little shelter of

any kind. Thousands of Indians died along the way--
this was a bad time. I kept asking myself how could
this have happened. Clearly, President Jackson and
the Indian Removal Act were at the heart of the cause.
But how could people let this happen?

Deceptions / Ruthlessness

Our government is very good at making people believe something when they themselves do not. They
are very good at lying and altering the facts in order to
get what they want without regard to the consequences. Two centuries ago in dealing with the Cherokee
and Natives, the US government, during Andrew
Jackson's presidency, used deception, lies, bribes, li-
quor, and manipulation to steal Cherokee and Native
lands. In my company's example, the Small Business
Administration lied, telling the world that they never
gave federal government contracts set aside for small
businesses to big businesses claiming to be small business. The "Gulf of Tonkin" incident which proceeded
the war in Viet Nam was a lie told to the American
public. There was never an incident, yet President
Johnson ordered US bombers to retaliate for an attack
that never happened. It allowed him to goad Congress
into escalating the Viet Nam War.

The US government lied to the American people, telling

them there was no conspiracy against Martin Luther King, Jr. The FBI was always critical of people who criticized their actions. During the 1950s, the FBI fought dissenters, through a covert program called COINTELPRO. The mission was to "disrupt, discredit, or otherwise neutralize" disobedient people and groups.

During the COINTELPRO period, the FBI managed thousands subversive smear operations. The FBI tapped phones, forged papers, to create negative public image of dissenters.

After MLK gave his famous "I Have a Dream" speech, this memo floated through FBI offices:

> *"In the light of King's powerful demagogic speech yesterday he stands heads and shoulders over all other Negro leaders put together when it comes to influencing great masses of Negros. We must mark him now, if we have not done so before, as the most dangerous Negro of the future in this nation from the standpoint of communism, the Negro, and national security."*

MLK was classified an unofficial Enemy of State. The FBI tracked his every movement around the country. The objective was to neutralize MLK as an effective Negro leader.

Jackson went so far as to suggest to the Cherokee that they would be happier living among their own in land west of the Mississippi, because the Cherokee would not like living among the Euro people. In his speech before the US Congress December 6, 1830, Jackson called the Cherokee "savage hunters." He talked about making the Cherokee people happy and prosperous. He neglected to mention that the Cherokee had built cabins to live in, built schools, and had successful working farms and other businesses before contact with the European settlers. Jackson wanted to separate Indians from the Euros to advance the state rapidly in population, wealth, and power. Owning the Cherokee land was the best way to do this.

President Jackson was a master at communications and convincing the public to see things his way. Jackson was a person who clearly understood political power and behavior. He used it well. He was cruel and ruthless toward the Cherokee and Native Indians. When people live under a government that lies to you, it becomes impossible to know anything for certain about your life. The only thing you know for sure is what the government tells you. Like President Jackson, the SBA has done a masterful job in keeping small business and the public blind or in the dark as to how SBA are preventing federal government set-aside contracts from going to small business.

Small Business Information:

Federal regulators exempt GSA Schedule contracts from small-business set- asides, despite congressional mandate in the Small Business Act, which states that all federal acquisitions in the simplified acquisition threshold (contracts valued between $3,000 and $150,000) must be set aside for small businesses. The SBA and FAR council essentially repealed this valuable piece of legislation by exempting all acquisitions on the GSA schedule from small-business set-asides.

CHAPTER **9**

What is a Lie / What is the Truth

"Make the lie big, make it simple, keep saying it, and eventually they will believe it."

- (Unknown)

We as Americans are the most lied-to people on earth. Americans in the 18th century and in the 21st century think they are free in this country--don't believe it; the government still can do pretty much whatever it wants. It did it with the Cherokee land grab, and today it is doing it with stealing small-business contracts. We are a nation that is clueless about what is going on in the world today. I have often said to myself when people say, "the ugly American" what they really mean is that we as Americans are clueless. In order for a government to be successful in lying to its people, it is important that they not tell the truth. Don't teach true history and what really happened in schools and educational institutions.

I believe the reason so many Americans are clueless is directly related to our educational system. I remember when I was in school I truly was not taught anything about the Cherokee and the Trail of Tears and the impact on America in removing Cherokee from their ancestry homeland in the southeastern part of the United States to Oklahoma. Clearly, the effort to send Cherokee to the west of the Mississippi river was because most Euros wanted their land and did not see development (civilization) taking place in the west any time soon; therefore, it made perfect sense to ship the Cherokee and other natives to Oklahoma. How wrong they were.

A government that lies to the people stops being a lawful government of the land. A government that lies in order to steal land from the Indian to give to wealthy Euro farmers and settlers is telling some of the worst possible lies a government can commit against its people. A government that does so without the consent of the governed is wrong. We are a nation founded on the principle of rule with the consent of the governed. America's policies toward Native Americans have been filled with broken promises and lies. Our government still is untrustworthy and dangerous. Nothing has changed from 200 years ago.

The driving force is still driven by powerful men and money. We trust our government to do the right thing and they don't. We as Americans should be angry, be in a rage over our government telling us lies. As long as the public remains silent, our government will continue to tell us lies. As long as we remain silent, the liars haven't any reason to stop.

> *"America has gone from a nation of laws to a nation Of powerful men making laws in secret accountable to Only power and money."*
>
> - (Unknown)

CHAPTER 10

European Settlers Hungry for Cherokee Land

The Cherokee and Natives, in the opinion of many European settlers, were standing in the way of making money or making progress. These Euros were made up primarily of farmers who wanted the land to raise cotton and tobacco. They pressured the federal government to acquire the Indian land. In the case of the Cherokee, they might have been able to fight the renegade settlers and farmers for a long time. However, two factors stood in the way. Andrew Jackson became president in 1828; and in 1830, the Indian Removal Act was passed, and gold was found on Cherokee lands in Georgia.

Needless to say, at this point it was all over for the Indians ownership of their land. The tide of settlers from Georgia, Carolina, Virginia, and Alabama seeking wealth on Indian property could not be stopped. President Jackson enjoyed this invasion of Cherokee land. He had created numerous treaties making it easy to steal Indian property.

Andrew Jackson didn't care about rights of the Cherokee or Native--to him, they were not considered citizens. Jackson wanted all Euro men to be able to vote. During this period only property owners could vote. Jackson's actions were clearly self-serving. Promises and treaties were almost always broken. Many Euros saw the Indians as "savages" and uncivilized--what they really were saying was Indians were not or did not do or think as European people. Jackson wrote, "Those tribes cannot exist surrounded by our settlements. They have neither the intelligence nor the moral habits...established in the midst of a superior race. They must disappear."

What arrogance, what a superiority complex Jackson had! He was truly a man who had strong confidence in himself, to accomplish what he did. He had a self-importance few could match. Actually, this attitude of Jackson's should not be surprising. After the War of 1812 in which Jackson was a general, and was the first president arrested by the British, he called for the government to end the "absurdity" of negotiating with the Indian tribes as sovereign nations.

It is interesting to note the racial attitude of powerful men toward the Indians during this period in American history, given the heavy discrimination toward the Indians on the part of the Euro settlers and farmers. Euro settlers, particularly those who lived on the western frontier, often feared and resented the Native Americans they encountered.

Many high-level bureaucrats in the early years of America, such as President George Washington, believed that the best way to solve the "Indian problem" was simply to "civilize" the Native Americans. His objective was to make the Indians enlightened according to European standards, to make Native Americans as much like Euro Americans as possible by encouraging them to adapt to Christianity, learn to speak and read English, and adopt European-style ways of living--for example, individual ownership of land and other property, including owning African slaves.

Washington gave a farm to Major John Ridge and a spinning wheel to his wife for looming. He wanted them to learn the European way. Washington, however, was like many other Americans at the time--they were unfamiliar with how advanced the Indians were in these areas, particularly in the south along the Mississippi. The bulk of the Indians lived in a town with streets and buildings. They had a structured government ruled by chiefdoms (kinship-based). They also had a legal system for owning slaves. This is one case when Washington was bringing up the rear.

In the southeastern United States, many Choctaw, Chickasaw, Seminole, Creek, and Cherokee people embraced these customs and became known as the Five Civilized Tribes. They were successful farmers, and built schools; they governed themselves much like the Americans. They even dressed like some European Americans. The Cherokee had a government and built a capital. They were prosperous. This made many Euros anxious to have the Native land. It also increased the Euro hatred for the Cherokee. Unfortunately for the Cherokee, Washington's ideas were not widely accepted by Euro America. It's worth pointing out that the Chickasaw received compensation from the United States--approximately $530,000 or over $11 million dollars in today's value for their land east of the Mississippi river.

Small Business Information

Large corporations and federal contracting officers are not being punished for missing their small-business procurement goals and are not being prosecuted for fraudulent contracting.

- *Existing federal laws, known as "liquidated*

damages clauses," establish penalties for prime contractors when they are non-compliant with small-business goals. Because this law has never been enforced by the SBA and Department of Justice, most prime contractors never achieve the small-business goals required in their federal contracts.

■ *Current federal law establishes that misrepresenting the size of a firm in order to illegally receive federal contracts and subcontracts is a felony with penalties of up to 10 years in prison, a fine up to $500,000, cancellation of all contracts, and debarment from selling to the government. Federal policy should require the SBA to respond to any protest against any firm that misrepresents its size, regardless of whether or not the contract is a small business set-aside. Section 16(d) of federal code makes no differentiation as to the type of the contract; therefore current SBA policy is illegal and does not address the magnitude of the problem.*

Indian Removal Act of 1830

The Indian Removal Act of 1830 was the biggest nightmare the Cherokee faced 200 years ago. It represented the end of a proud people and their way of life whose only fault was their desire to live in peace on their ancestral land. Most Americans like myself had not realized that Indian Removal took place in northern states as well--Illinois and Wisconsin are prime examples. The Black Hawk War in 1832 opened to Euro settlement millions of acres of land that had belonged to the Sauk, Fox, and other Native nations.

However, their land, located in parts of Georgia, Alabama, North Carolina, Florida, and Tennessee, was valuable, and it grew to be more desirable as Euro settlers flooded the region. Many of these Euro yearned to make their riches by growing cotton. They did not care how "civilized" their Native neighbors were. They wanted that land, and they would do anything to get it. There were reports of Euro settlers stealing livestock, burning and looting houses and towns, and squatting on land that did not belong to them.

This period in American history was one of the worst times imaginable for the Cherokee and Natives. Euro settlers--never losing sight of their objective of taking Cherokee land--put strong pressure on the government, where a friendly ear existed in then-President Andrew Jackson, to do something. Jackson encouraged state governments to join in this effort to drive Native Americans out of the South. Several states passed laws limiting Native American sovereignty and rights, and encroaching on their territory.

> *"My father was the first to see through the schemes of the white men....He said: 'My son...when I am gone...you are the chief of these people....Always remember that your father never sold his country....This country holds your father's body. Never sell the bones of your father and mother.' I pressed my father's hand and told him I would protect his grave with my life....A man who would not love his father's grave is worse than a wild animal."*

>   - Chief Joseph

The Debate over the Cherokee Removal

President Jackson's message to Congress as it began to debate the Indian Removal Act that would give him the power to remove the Cherokee and all Native Americans west of the Mississippi River:

> *It gives me pleasure to announce to Congress that the benevolent policy of the Government, steadily pursued for nearly thirty years, in relation to the removal of the Indians beyond the white settlements is approaching to a happy consummation.*

> *Two important tribes have accepted the provision made for their removal at the last session of*

Congress, and it is believed that their example will induce the remaining tribes also to seek the same obvious advantages.

The consequences of a speedy removal will be important to the United States, to individual States, and to the Indians themselves. The pecuniary [monetary] advantages which it promises to the Government are the least of its recommendations. It puts an end to all possible dangers of collision between the authorities of the General and State Governments on account of the Indians.

It will place a dense and civilized population in large tracts of a country now occupied by a few savage hunters. By opening the whole territory between Tennessee on the north and Louisiana on the south to the settlement of the whites it will incalculably strengthen the southwestern frontier and render the adjacent States strong enough to repel future invasions without a remote aid.

It will relieve the whole State of Mississippi and the western part of Alabama of Indian occupancy, and enable those States to advance rapidly in population, wealth, and power. It will separate the Indians from immediate contact with settlements of whites; free them from the power of the States; enable them to pursue happiness in their own way and under their own rude institutions; I will retard the progress of decay, which is lessening their numbers, and perhaps cause them gradually, under the protection of the Government and through the influence of good counsels, to cast off their savage habits and become an interesting, civilized, and Christian community. . . . President Andrew Jackson

Memorial of the Cherokee Nation, 1830:

"We wish to remain on the land of our fathers. We have a perfect and original right to remain without interruption or molestation. The treaties with us, and laws of the United States made in pursuance of treaties, guaranty our residence and our privileges, and secure us against intruders. Our only request is, that these treaties may be fulfilled, and these laws executed. But if we are compelled to leave our country, we see nothing but ruin before us. The country west of the Arkansas territory is unknown to us." (Reprint from "Memorial of the Cherokee Nation," in Nile's Weekly Register, 1830).

Indian Removal Act--Sadness: In the 18th century and early part of the 19th century, many Native American treaties were signed giving the US government Indian land. The purpose was to make available the land to Euro settlers and farmers. In addition, a significant part of northern Georgia was open to gold mining. The government was concerned with protection, which was always an issue with the US Government. These treaties offered a buffer between Americans and the Spanish and others in the west.

In his inaugural address, President Andrew Jackson, in 1829 set forth his policy of relocating all the Indians in the southeastern United States. The Indian Removal Act of 1830 was signed on May 26, 1830 by President Andrew Jackson. This law would have made former President Thomas Jefferson happy. When he purchased the Louisiana Territory from France in 1803, it gave him the opportunity to implement his idea to relocate the Indian Tribes beyond the Mississippi River. The Indian Removal Act cemented his and President Jackson's ideas for relocating the Indians.

The legislation, which Jackson fought hard for, authorizes the federal government to negotiate treaties with eastern tribes, exchanging their land for land in the west across the Mississippi heading toward Oklahoma or Indian Territory. The Act gave the government a legal justification for the wholesale and forceful removal of the Cherokee. This law was designed to make it easy to remove the Cherokee and the other Natives off their land. Even though many Cherokee approved the treaties requiring them to be removed from their homeland to west of the Mississippi, many did not want to leave their ancestral homeland.

While treaties existed between the federal government and the Cherokee, what comes into question is the way the government took the land from the Indians, lying to the Indians, using and creating laws to fit the Euro settlers' and states' positions, creating treaties and creating questionable justification to make those treaties fit their purpose. It is interesting to note that in 1787, the Northwest Ordinance stated that Indians were to be treated with the *"utmost good faith"* and *"their lands and property shall never be taken away from them without their consent."* However, as settlers moved into occupied Indian Territory, they had to receive military guard.

When the Europeans arrived on America's shores, the Cherokee controlled a large area of land, well over twenty million acres in eight different states. By 1830, the Cherokee had given up most of their land. The Indian Removal Act was surrounded with controversy. Many Americans did not support the Removal Act for many different reasons. Christian missionaries, who lived and worked with the Indians for years, were opposed to the Act. They felt it would lead to giving southern farmers the power to expand a slavery-based agriculture into newly acquired lands.

Others opposed the Act. It became an issue dealing with giving more power to the federal government over state rights. The Indian Removal Act was debated heavily in Congress before passing; it was not unanimously supported, however. Senators Daniel Webster and Henry Clay and others opposed the Act. Many treaties with the Indians involved their giving up land in the East in exchange for land in the Indian Territory. The exchanges were never equal. The tribe gave up more than they received.

Small Business Information - *A brief look at the problem*

When discussing the diversion of federal small business contracts to large corporations, most people are amazed to find out that a foreign company with 26,000 employees with offices in 17 countries has been considered a small business in the past and has received federal small business contracts. However, the reality of the matter is that the problem is not one large company receiving federal small business contracts, but dozens. ASBL estimates that roughly $60 billion a year in federal small business contracts is diverted to large corporations.

One of the big problems small businesses have is getting government contracting officers to believe that they are capable of doing the job. Many government contracting officers say things like "They are too small," "They don't have the experience," "They don't understand the small business complexities of the contract process." The regulations and policies that administrate this process can be difficult to negotiate. A small business cannot grow if they don't have the opportunity. Government contracting officers should follow the law and make sure that small contractors get the set-aside contracts set aside for them.

CHAPTER 11

Who Was Andrew Jackson - What Were His True Colors?

Andrew Jackson, was the seventh president of the United States of America. He was born in a backwoods settlement in the Waxhaw area, to a poor farming family between the borders of North and South Carolina on March 15, 1767. He studied law for a little over two years and was considered a pretty good lawyer. Many people thought he had a quick temper and was quick to get into brawls. He is reported to have dueled with a man and killed him over a comment the man made about his wife.

Jackson prospered sufficiently as a planter to purchase a good number of slaves (300) and build a mansion, The Hermitage near Nashville, on 1000 acres. He served in the House of Representatives and for a short time in the Senate. Actually, Jackson was the first Congressman from Tennessee. He was elected president in 1828. He made his reputation as a military leader during the war of 1812 with England, the Creek War of 1814 and the Seminole Indian War of 1818. Jackson was called King Andrew I. Unlike other presidents, Jackson did not defer to Congress in policy-making. He used his power to veto and his party leadership to get what he wanted.

Jackson clearly was a president who would not take no for an answer or allow any opposition to what he wanted. He was used to getting his way. It explains how he was able to get the Indian Removal Act passed through Congress. There are many examples to justify why Jackson was called King Andrew I, such as the battle of the second Bank of the United States, a private corporation, but a government- sponsored monopoly. When Jackson became hostile, the bank threw its power against him. Sen. Clay and Sen. Webster acted as attorneys for the bank, and led the fight in Congress for re-charter. Jackson is reported to have said to Martin Van Buren, "The bank is trying to kill me, but I will kill it." Jackson vetoed the re-charter bill and charged the bank with undue economic privilege. His view won the approval of the American electorate in 1832; he polled more than 56 % of the popular vote--substantially more than Clay.

John C. Calhoun was leader of those trying to rid themselves of high protective tariff, Jackson decided to take this issue head on. Jackson ordered troops to Charleston and threated to hang Calhoun. Violence seemed imminent until Clay negotiated a compromise. Tariffs were lowered and South Carolina dropped nullification.

One only has to wonder what the Cherokee life would be like if Richard Lawrence had carried out his plan to kill President Jackson. Jackson claims the distinction of being the first American president to survive a presidential assassination attempt--on January 30, 1835. Lawrence's gun misfired twice and Jackson unarmed the gunman. Jackson is also credited with helping to create the state of Tennessee.

I have given the reader more information on Jackson, because of his impact on the Indian Removal Act, and the Trail of Tears. He is directly responsible for the death of over 4000 Cherokee during their march to Oklahoma from the southeastern United States. He is responsible for hurt and death to peaceful people who only wanted to live their lives on their land.

In 1835, Andrew Jackson, submitted a new treaty to the Cherokee National Council. In doing so he stated:

"I have long viewed your condition with great interest. For many years, I have become acquainted with your people, and under all variety of circumstances in peace and war. You are now placed in the midst of a white population. Your peculiar customs, which regulated your intercourse with one another, have been abrogated by the great political community among which you live, and you are now subject to the same laws which govern the other citizens of Georgia and Alabama.

I have no motive, my friends, to deceive you. I am sincerely desirous to promote your welfare. Listen to me; therefore, while I tell you that you cannot remain where you now are. Circumstances that cannot be controlled, and, which are beyond the reach of human laws, render it impossible that you can flourish in the midst of a civilized community. You have but one remedy within your reach. And that is, to remove to the west and join your countrymen, who are already established there. And the sooner you do this the sooner you will commence your career of improvement and prosperity."

This speech and its contents were lies, and misleading.

Jackson could not be trusted, and he was clearly dangerous to the Cherokee.

Between the years of 1814 to 1824, Jackson was instrumental in negotiating nine out of eleven treaties, which took the southern tribes off their eastern lands. When Jackson took away the Cherokee lands, he was the prime example of American political corruption. He used his power as a government official to illegally obtain private gains for himself and Euro settlers. Jackson broke many different laws. As an office-holder, what he did constituted political corruption because his actions were directly related to his official duties. 200 years later, our government uses the same practice to steal small-business contracts and give them to big business claiming to be small business.

Small Business Information

The SBA has a policy of excluding small businesses from eligibility for $100 billion worth of federal contracts from the acquisitions budget, which violates the Congressional intent of the Small Business Act, which clearly states that small businesses must receive 23 % of total federal prime contracts.

Opposition to the Indian Removal Act

As I mentioned earlier, there were many Cherokee who opposed the Indian Removal Act. Chief John Ross was perhaps the best-known Cherokee tribal chief who opposed the Indian Removal Act of 1830. Chief Ross believed that the Cherokee should fight through the white man's system, using political and legal methods to resolve the Cherokee land removal question. He was highly respected for the way he handled the Indian Removal Issue. Before 1838, Chief Ross was one of the richest men in northern Georgia. He owned over 200 acres of farm land and a number of slaves. However, he wasn't comfortable speaking the Cherokee language in public. He was highly educated and studied the law.

Ross honestly believed that the Cherokee would be treated fairly by the Euro system of justice. His faith in the Republican form of government, and the authority of the US Supreme Court, along with the political power of Cherokee supporters, gave him confidence that the Cherokee rights would be protected. When the Treaty of New Echota, named after the Cherokee capital, which was established in 1825, was authorized by one vote in the US Senate in 1836, Ross continued to believe that Euro America would not eject the most "civilized" native people in the Southeast. How wrong he was.

It is sad, given the attitude of many Euros and Euro settlers during this period toward the Cherokee, that Chief John Ross could not see his approach would not work. It is a dilemma--sometimes the truth is painful and sad. Ross was a mixed-blood Cherokee who was very popular among the Cherokee, particularly with the traditional Cherokee. He was familiar with English and spoke it. He was familiar with the American law. He tried his best to live the European way of life without losing his Cherokee culture and identity. Between the years of 1830 and 1838, he made numerous trips to Washington to plead the cause of his people to stay on their homeland. He found little support from Congress and no support from the president, often getting the response that "there is nothing they can do." He finally turned to the courts, ending up in the Supreme Court. (Cherokee Nation v. Georgia 1831.)

The first major case that the Cherokee brought before the court in 1831 was Cherokee Nation v._Georgia. The case involved a dispute over Georgia's attempt to extend its jurisdiction over Cherokee territory. Chief Justice John Marshall denies Indians the right to court protection because they are not subject to the laws of the constitution. He describes Indian tribes as "domestic dependent nations," saying that each is "a distinct political entity…capable of managing its own affairs."

Small Business Information:

Federal regulators exempt GSA Schedule contracts from small-business set-asides, despite Congressional mandate in the Small Business Act, which states that all federal acquisitions in the simplified acquisition threshold (contracts valued between $3,000 and $150,000) must be set aside for small businesses. The SBA and FAR council essentially repealed this valuable piece of legislation by exempting all acquisitions on the GSA schedule from small- business set-asides.

Agencies like to use the set-aside SBA contracting program because it helps the agencies meet their 23% goal.

Worcester v. Georgia 1832 – Chief John Ross – Seminole Tribe

Between the 1820s and 1830s, Georgia conducted a relentless campaign to remove the Cherokee from their land in the state. Feeling this pressure, in 1827 the Cherokee decided to establish a constitutional government and declared to the American public that they were a sovereign nation who could not be relocated without their permission. The Georgia legislature was angry and declared boundaries over Cherokee living in the state. The state annexed the

Cherokee lands, and abolished their government and laws. The state established a law for seizing Cherokee land and distributing it to Euro citizens.

Chief John Ross refused to move, and filed an action with the Supreme Court questioning the constitutional support of Georgia's law. The argument of the Cherokee was a good one. They argued Georgia's law violated their sovereign rights as a nation and illegally intruded into their treaty relationship with the American government.

Samuel Worcester was a missionary living among the Cherokee, who worked closely with Cherokee leaders and had advised them on their rights in the constitution and federal Cherokee treaties. He was a friend of Chief John Ross. Worcester was a native of Vermont, and he was affiliated with the American Board of Commissioners for Foreign Missions. The Georgia government recognized Worcester's and other missionaries' importance to Cherokee resistance and passed a law banning Euro persons from Cherokee territory if they had not first declared their loyalty toward the state of Georgia, as of March 1, 1831. Any Euro wishing to be on Cherokee land, working or having residency, must have a license. Worcester and several others disobeyed the law and was arrested. He was released because he was the Postmaster of Echota. The Governor of Georgia got him fired and eleven days later, the state of Georgia arrested Worcester and other missionaries for violating the law again. Worcester was sent to prison for four years' hard labor. He was later pardoned by the new Governor of Georgia, and he left the state.

The US Supreme Court objected to the practices of the state of Georgia and affirmed that Native nations were sovereign nations "in which the laws of Georgia and other states can have no force." Chief Justice Marshall eventually seemed to support the legal arguments of the Cherokee and Native. He supported the argument that the jurisdiction over the Cherokee belonged to the federal government, not the states. He wrote that the Cherokee constituted a "domestic dependent nation" that existed under the guardianship of the United States. President Andrew Jackson ignored the ruling and encouraged Georgia to keep harassing the Cherokee, which it did.

President Andrew Jackson, in response to the court's decision is reputed to have said, "*John Marshall has made his decision. Now let him enforce it.*" There isn't any conformation that Jackson actually said this. It should be pointed out, in all fairness to President Jackson, that it would have been hard for the US Government to enforce Marshall's decision when they were not part of the suit and neither were the Cherokee. Worcester did not have any obligation on Jackson; there were nothing to enforce. Neither the court nor Worcester requested Jackson's help and Marshall did not requested that Jackson enforce his decision.

What we know for sure is that Jackson did nothing to enforce the law or Marshall's decision. Jackson saw the Cherokee as annoying irritation, and he wanted to get rid of them. He supported any state law or treaties designed to take land from them.

Even with this ruling, the abuses continued against the Cherokee. Jackson is reported to have stated in 1832 that if no one intended to enforce the Supreme Court's rulings (which he certainly did not), then the decisions would "[fall]…still born." Southern states were determined to take ownership of Indian lands and would go to great lengths to secure the territory. One tribe that rejected outright forced removal was the **Seminole tribe** in Florida. The first Seminole war was in 1817 to 1818, over land issues. The Seminole were supported by large numbers of fugitive slaves who found protection among the Seminole. The presence of the fugitive slaves enraged many Euro planters and fueled their desires to defeat the Seminole.

In 1833, a group of Seminole were tricked into signing a treaty calling for their removal. This act brought about a second Seminole war between 1835 and 1842. Thousands of lives were lost in the war, which was reported to have cost the US government between $40 and $60 million dollars. A third war took place during 1855 to 1858. In each of the Cherokee wars, fugitive slaves placed a big role. Finally, the US government got tired of fighting and paid the Seminole a reported large sum to go west, which many did.

CHAPTER 12

Chief Justice John Marshall

Excerpts from the Majority Opinion in Worcester v. Georgia 1832

MARSHALL, C. J. This cause, in every point of view in which it can be placed, is of the deepest interest. The defendant is a State, a member of the Union, which has exercised the powers of government over a people who deny its jurisdiction, and are under the protection of the United States.

The plaintiff is a citizen of the State of Vermont, condemned to hard labor for four years in the penitentiary of Georgia under color of an act which he alleges to be repugnant to the Constitution, laws, and treaties of the United States.

The legislative power of a State, the controlling power of the Constitution and laws of the United States, the rights, if they have any, the political existence of once numerous and powerful people, the personal liberty of a citizen, all are involved in the subject now to be considered. . . .

We must inquire and decide whether the act of the Legislature of Georgia under which the plaintiff in error has been persecuted and condemned, be consisted with, or repugnant to the Constitution, laws and treaties of the United States.

It has been said at the bar that the acts of the Legislature of Georgia seize on the whole Cherokee country, parcel it out among the neighboring counties of the State, extend her code over the whole country, abolish its institutions and its laws, and annihilate its political existence.

If this be the general effect of the system, let us inquire into the effect of the particular statute and section on which the indictment is founded.

It enacts that "all white persons, residing within the limits of the Cherokee Nation on the 1st day of March next, or at any time thereafter, without a license or permit from his excellency the governor . . . and who shall not have taken the oath hereinafter required, shall be guilty of a high misdemeanor, and upon conviction thereof, shall be punished by confinement to the penitentiary at hard labor for a term not less than four years." . . .

The extraterritorial power of every Legislature being limited in its action to its own citizens or subjects, the very passage of this act is an assertion of jurisdiction over the Cherokee Nation, and of the rights and powers consequent on jurisdiction. The first step, then, in the inquiry which the Constitution and the laws impose on this court, is an examination of the rightfulness of this claim. . .

From the commencement of our government Congress has passed acts to regulate trade and intercourse with the Indians; which treat them as nations, respect their rights, and manifest a firm purpose to afford that protection which treaties stipulate. All these acts, and especially that of 1802, which is still in force, manifestly consider the several Indian nations as distinct political communities, having territorial boundaries, within which their authority is exclusive, and having

A right to all the lands within those boundaries, which is not only acknowledged, but guaranteed by the United States. . . .

The Cherokee Nation, then, is a distinct community, occupying its own territory, with boundaries accurately described, in which the laws of Georgia can have no force, and which the citizens of Georgia have no right to enter but with the assent of the Cherokee themselves or in conformity with treaties and with the acts of Congress. The whole intercourse between the United States and this nation is, by our Constitution and laws, vested in the government of the United States.

The act of the State of Georgia under which the plaintiff in error was prosecuted is consequently, void, and the judgment a nullity. . . . The Acts of Georgia are repugnant to the Constitution, laws, and treaties of the United States.

They interfere forcibly with the relations established between the United States and the Cherokee Nation, the regulation of which according to the settled

Principles of our Constitution, are committed exclusively to the government of the Union.

They are in direct hostility with treaties, repeated in a succession of years, which mark out the boundary that separates the Cherokee country from Georgia; guarantee to them all the land within their boundary; solemnly pledge the faith of the United States to restrain their citizens from trespassing on it; and recognize the pre-existing power of the nation to govern itself.

They are in equal hostility with the acts of Congress for regulating this intercourse, and giving effect to the treaties. The forcible seizure and abduction of the plaintiff, who was residing in the nation with its permission, and by authority of the President of the United States, is also a violation of the acts which authorize the chief magistrate to exercise this authority. . . . *Judgment reversed.*

Who Was John Marshall?

John Marshall served as Chief Justice of the Supreme Court between the years 1801 and 1835. He was born September 24, 1755 and died July 6, 1835. He is credited with his opinion to have helped the United States Constitutional law and made the judicial branch equal to the executive and legislative branches of government.

Marshall had knowledge about the Congress, since he served in the US House of Representative from 1799 to 1800. He was a leader of the Federalist Party from Virginia. From the years of 1800 to 1801, he served under President John Adams, as secretary of state, before Adams made him chief justice in what became known as the Midnight Judge Act, in which Congress made sweeping changes to the judiciary in one night while confirming Marshall as chief justice. Marshall became the longest-serving chief justice in the history of the court--34 years.

Marshall could match intellectual keenness or stand up to any political opponent of his day. Many of his decisions did not sit well or were unpopular. However, he built the court and is credited for augmented federal power under the name of the constitution and the rule of law. He made the court an independent branch of government. He repeatedly confirmed the supremacy of federal law over state law. He supported an expansive reading of enumerated powers (a list of items found in Article 1, Section 8 of the US Constitution that deals with the authoritative capacity of Congress).

Marshall and Daniel Webster, were friends and Webster argued a number of cases before the court. As Federalist leaders, they fought to build a stronger federal government in contrast to Jeffersonian Republicans who wanted a stronger state government. It is easy to see how President Andrew Jackson, disliked Marshall. It is also clear how Marshall reached his the decision in Worcester v. Georgia 1832, impacting the Cherokee. I think the thinking of States Right verses Federal Right had to cross his mind. President John Adams stated, "My gift of John Marshall to the people of the United States was the proudest act of my life."

CHIEF JUSTICE JOHN MARSHALL ❧

In later years Marshall felt his decision in Johnson v. M'Intosh, 1823 may have set the foundation for the Trail of Tears. This case involved the court landmark decision in which it held that private citizens could not purchase land from Native Americans. The court held "Johnson's lessees cannot eject M'Intosh because their title, derived from private purchases from Native Americans, could not be valid." Many of Marshall's friends felt the language in his Fletcher and Johnson decision, had been used as justification for Georgia's action.

Small businesses still cry out for justice asking. When will the courts look at how the federal government is violating contract law impacting the small business ability to obtain federal government contracts set aside for their business?

Small Business Information

Alaska Native Corporations receive special preference that has led to ANCs acquiring a monopoly on federal small business contracts, especially contracts meant for all tribal firms [8(a) contracts], and contracts for small disadvantaged businesses.

From the 1980s to the early 1990s, Congress passed a series of laws that made Alaska Native

Corporations eligible for federal contracting opportunities as socially and economically disadvantaged minority-owned businesses, including the SBA's 8(a) program. These laws also gave ANCs contracting preferences that no other socio-economic demographic possesses, such as the ability to receive no-bid federal contracts of unlimited value, remain in the 8(a) program indefinitely, and have multiple 8(a) subsidiaries.

By now, the regulatory and legislative preferences that ANCs possess have allowed ANCs to manipulate the 8(a) and SBD programs for their own overwhelming success, and pass their profits to their non-Native executive and non-Native subcontractors. A report conducted in 2009 by Senator Claire McCaskill stated, **"Alaska Native Corporations are multi-million or billion dollar corporations that are now among the largest federal contractors. Although ANCs provide some benefit to their shareholders, those benefits may not be in proportion to the potential for waste, fraud and abuse created by the ANCs contracting preferences."**

Other findings in Senator McCaskill's report showed:

- *ANCs are currently among the top 100 largest federal contractors.*

- *The majority of ANCs are big businesses.*
- *Alaska Native Corporations "have taken advantage of the exemption from size requirements to create multiple 8(a) subsidiaries." Between 2000 and 2008, the 19 ANCs surveyed by McCaskill's staff enrolled 248 subsidiaries, joint ventures or partnerships in the 8(a) program.*
- *Alaska Native Corporations may be passing work through to subcontractors, many of which are large, non-Native companies.*
- *ANCs employ a small %age of shareholders. The 2009 study from Senator McCaskill found that "on average, nearly 95% of ANC employees are not ANC shareholders."*
- *Alaska Native Corporations "have relied heavily on highly-paid, non-Native executives."*

Chief John Ross Negotiations

Principal Chief John Ross continued negotiations with the federal government on behalf of the Cherokee. Between 1833 and 1835, Ross made numerous proposals regarding solutions to the problem, including sale of part of the Cherokee lands for Cherokee to have the same rights as Euros, like the right to vote, own property, hold office, and the right to testify at trial. Needless to say, this proposal was rejected. Ross proposed a second suggestion in which he offered to sell all Cherokee holdings for $20 million. It was too late--the state of Georgia had taken nearly all the Cherokee land by this time. In 1835, a few hundred Cherokee met in New Echota, Georgia, which was the capital of Cherokee Nation, to sign a new treaty. This minority faction of the Cherokee organized the Treaty Party and began negotiations with the US government. This was an elected group with no authority. They believed removal was inevitable, and they signed the New Echota Treaty with the federal government. The Cherokee would receive payment of five million dollars for all the land east of the Mississippi river given to the US government, and the Cherokee would receive new western homelands.

Echota Treaty

The New Echota Treaty, was presented to the Cherokee National Council, and it was rejected. It was then presented to a general meeting of Cherokee where it received 114 votes out of over a thousand Cherokee who was present in attendance. Major John Ridge, who also worked with Andrew Jackson during the War of 1812, was the key supporter of the treaty. He and the other leaders of the Treaty Party signed the document, and the federal government narrowly ratified the treaty. Chief John Ross tried to organize the Cherokee against it, and failed to stop the implementation.

On April 6, 1838, General Winfield Scott arrived in Georgia with 7000 troops to enforce the treaty to relocate over 15,000 Cherokee to Oklahoma. He designated May 26, 1838 as the start date for the first phase of the removal. He began the process of rounding up all the Indians (Cherokee), putting them in rat-infected stockades with little food, water, or blankets in the internment camp. These people had to march over 1000 miles, many barefoot. Many suffered from measles and smallpox. Over 4,000 Indians died. The survivors in 1839 call the march the Trail of Tears. One of those who died was Chief John Ross' wife Quatie (also known as Elizabeth Brown Henley).

Major John Ridge – Echota Treaty: In December 1835, Major Ridge spoke of his reason for supporting the Echota Treaty. Ridge, was part of a group of Cherokee who felt it served no purpose to continue fighting for their land. Major Ridge, felt that the only way for the Cherokee to survive as a nation was to move. He felt strongly about this issue and in 1832, he felt accepting removal of the Cherokee should at least be compensated. Ridge and a group of friends and relatives presented their proposal to the Cherokee National Council in October 1832. It was defeated. Chief John Ross, was the voice of the majority opposing any further cessions of land.

In December 1835, the US resubmitted the treaty to

a meeting of 300 to 500 Cherokee at New Echota. Older now, Major Ridge spoke of his reasons for supporting the treaty:

"I am one of the native sons of these wild woods. I have hunted the deer and turkey here, more than fifty years. I have fought your battles, have defended your truth and honesty, and fair trading.

The Georgians have shown a grasping spirit lately; they have extended their laws, to which we are unaccustomed, which harass our Braves and makes the children suffer and cry. I know the Indians have an older title than theirs.

We obtained the land from the living God his son above. They got their title from the British. Yet they are strong, and we are weak. We are few. They are many. We cannot remain here in safety and comfort. I know we love the graves of our fathers.

We can never forget these homes, but an unbending, iron necessity tells us we must leave them. I would willingly die to preserve them, but any forcible effort to keep them will cost us our lands, our lives and the lives of our children.

There is but one path of safety, one road to future existence as a Nation. That path is open before you. Make a treaty of a cession. Give up these lands and go over beyond the great father of Waters."

After Major Ridge signed The Treaty of New Echota in 1835, he said, "I have just signed my death warrant," and indeed, he had. Ridge, his son John, and nephew Elias lay dead within six months after the Cherokee arrival in the Oklahoma Territory in 1839. Ridge was shot while traveling to Arkansas on June 22, 1839. Not long after, a group of Cherokee dragged John Ridge from his home and stabbed him, it was reported, over 40 times in front of his wife and children. Elias Boudinot was murdered shortly after leaving Samuel Worcester's home. These men expected their death. The Cherokee National Council called for the death of anyone who agreed to give up tribal land. Most of the Treaty Party leaders were killed once they arrived in Oklahoma.

Over 100,000 Native Americans were forced to move between 1830 and 1869. The mass relocation caused untold suffering; it is estimated that over one-third died on the march from the East Coast to Indian Territory in Oklahoma. The reason for the death varied from a number of diseases, starvation, and cold weather (poor travelling conditions). It is estimated that the Indians left over 25 million acres of land to Euro settlement and to slavery on the East Coast.

The federal government lied and broke promises as usual when they told the Indians that their new land would remain unmolested forever. As the streak of Euro settlement pushed westward, "Indian territory" declined and declined. In 1907, Oklahoma became a state and oil was discovered, which attracted white speculators in large numbers. The Indian Territory was gone forever, never to return. Gone too was a proud and courageous people, their way of life and great cultural heritage.

Eyewitness Accounts: Those Who Witnessed the Trail of Tears

Editor Elias Boudinot, Who Opposes Indian Removal Act, 1828-Comment:

. . . Our last Washington papers contain a debate which took place in the House of Representatives, on the resolution, recommended by the Committee on Indian Affairs, published in the second Number of our paper.

It appears that the advocates of this new system of civilizing the Indians are very strenuous in maintaining the novel opinion, that it is impossible to enlighten the Indians, surrounded as they are by the white population, and that they assuredly will become extinct unless they are removed.

It is a fact which we would not deny, that many tribes have perished away in consequence of white population, but we are yet to be convinced that his will always be the case, in spite of every measure taken to civilize them.

We contend that suitable measures to a sufficient extent have never been employed. And how dare these men make an assertion without sufficient evidence? What proof have they that the system which they are now recommending, will succeed?

Where have we an example in the whole history of man, of a Nation or tribe removing in a body from a land of civil and religious means, to a perfect wilderness, in order to be civilized. We are fearful these men are building castles in the air, whose fall will crush those poor Indians who may be so blinded as to make the experiment.

We are sorry to see that some of the advocates of this system speak so disrespectfully, if not contemptuously, of the present measures of improvement, now in successful operation among the Indians in the United

States—the only measures too, which have been crowded with success and bid fair to meliorate the condition of the Aborigines . . .

John Burnett's Story of the Trail of Tears

John Burnett was an interpreter in the US Army during the Trail of Tears. In this letter to his children on his eightieth birthday in 1890, he recounts the painful journey, from the stockade experience to the end, and expresses his horror.

The removal of Cherokee Indians from their life long homes in the year of 1838 found me a young man in the prime of life and a Private soldier in the American Army.

Being acquainted with many of the Indians and able to fluently speak their language, I was sent as interpreter into the Smoky Mountain Country in May, 1838, and witnessed the execution of the most brutal order in the History of American Warfare. I saw the helpless Cherokee arrested and dragged from their homes, and driven at the bayonet point into the stockades. And in the chill of a drizzling rain on an October morning I saw them loaded like cattle or sheep into six hundred and forty-five wagons and started toward the west.

One can never forget the sadness and solemnity of

that morning. Chief John Ross led in prayer and when the bugle sounded and the wagons started rolling many of the children rose to their feet and waved their little hands good-by to their mountain homes, knowing they were leaving them forever. Many of these helpless people did not have blankets and many of them had been driven from home barefooted.

On the morning of November the 17th we encountered a terrific sleet and snow storm with freezing temperatures and from that day until we reached the end of the fateful journey on March the 26th, 1839, the sufferings of the Cherokee were awful.

The trail of the exiles was a trail of death. They had to sleep in the wagons and on the ground without fire. And I have known as many as twenty-two of them to die in one night of pneumonia due to ill treatment, cold, and exposure. Among this number was the beautiful Christian wife of Chief John Ross. This noble hearted woman died a martyr to childhood, giving her only blanket for the protection of a sick child.

She rode thinly clad through a blinding sleet and snow storm, developed pneumonia and died in the still hours of a bleak winter night, with her head resting on Lieutenant Greggs saddle blanket . . . The long painful journey to the west ended March 26th, 1839, with four thousand silent graves reaching from the foothills of the Smoky Mountains to what is known as Indian territory in the West. And covetousness on the part of the white race was the cause of all that the Cherokee had to suffer . . .

Traveler who signed himself "A Native of Maine," *The New York Observer*, **January 1839**

. . . On Tuesday evening we fell in with a detachment of the poor Cherokee Indians . . . about eleven hundred . . . We found them in the forest camped for the night . . . under a severe fall of rain . . . many of the aged Indians were suffering extremely from the fatigue of the journey, and ill health . . . We found the road literally filled with the procession for about three miles in length.

The sick and feeble were carried in wagons . . . multitudes go on foot — even aged females, apparently nearly ready to drop into the grave, were traveling with heavy burdens . . . on the sometimes frozen ground . . . with no covering for the feet . . . .They buried fourteen or fifteen at every stopping place . . . Some carry a downcast dejected look . . . of despair; others a wild frantic appearance as if about to . . . pounce like a tiger upon their enemies . . . When I read in the President's Message that he was happy to inform the Senate that the Cherokee were peaceably and without reluctance removed — and remember that it was on the third day of December when not one of the detachments had reached their destinations . . . I wished the President could have been there that very day . . .

Agnew, Mary Cobb-Comments:

May 25, 1937. An Interview with Mary Cobb Agnew; 917 North M Street; Muskogee, Oklahoma by Works Progress Administration Field Worker L.W. Wilson. (Wilson was part of a project to interview former slaves, American Indians and pioneer settlers.)

My name was Mary Cobb and I was married to Walter S. Agnew before the Civil War. I was born in Georgia on May 19, 1840. My mother was a Cherokee woman and my father was a white man. I was only four years old when my parents came to the Indian Territory and I am now 93 years old. My mother and father died when I was but seven years old and I was raised by an aunt, my mother's sister. I never attended school and my education is practical except what I was taught by my husband.

My parents did not come to the Territory on the "Trail of Tears," but my grandparents on my mother's side did. I have heard them say that the United States Government drove them out of Georgia. The Cherokee had protested to the bitter end. Finally, the Cherokee knew that they had to go someplace because the white men would kill their cattle and hogs and would even burn their houses in Georgia. The Cherokee came a group at a time until all got to the Territory.

They brought only a few things with them traveling by wagon train. Old men and women, sick men and women would ride, but most of them walked and the men in charge drove them like cattle, and many died on route and many other Cherokee died in Tennessee waiting to cross the Mississippi River. Dysentery broke out in their camp by the river, and many died, and many died on the journey, but my grandparents got through all right. I have heard my grandparents say that after they got out of the camp, and even before they left Georgia, many Cherokee were taken sick and later died. The Cherokee came through Tennessee, Kentucky, part of Missouri and then down to Indian Territory on the "Trail of Tears."

Some Cherokee were already in the country around Evansville, Arkansas, before my grandparents came. They called them Western Cherokee. It was in 1838 when my grandparents came and I heard them say it was in the winter time and all suffered with cold and hunger.

Support Documentation

1. John A. Russo, Jr., INS contracting officer letter to Shapleigh Drisco, SBA dated. May 16, 1996. This letter confirms the fact that INS had to notify SBA before executing any modification to the INS JCA contract

2. Blanket Purchasing Agreement dated 03/22/96, amount $25,000 signed by Lesa P. Scott, INS contracting officer. It shows J. Walter Thompson, claiming to be a Disadvantaged small business on government documentation

3. Blanket Purchasing Agreement dated 11/13/95, amount $7,062.15 signed by Betty Johnson, INS contracting officer. It confirms CASS Recruitment Publications. Stating they are disadvantaged small business on government documentation

4. Michelle Wall, INS contracting officer letter dated July 7, 1995 to SBA, Patricia Collins requesting permission to negotiate INS Letter Contract with JCA

5. Department of Justice Memorandum of Investigation dated July 15, 1997. It confirms INS knew that J. Walter Thompson, CASS Recruitment Publications and Bernard Hodes verified their small and disadvantaged business status to the INS Both the DOJ IG and the SBA IG knew from the investigative report that the contractors violated numerous SBA regulations along with the Business Opportunity Reform Act of 1988 (P.L. 100-656)

Sources
VᏧᏝᏙᎤ

Reprinted from "Memorial of the Cherokee Nation," in Nile's Weekly Register, 1830.

The CASE SBA Failure to Protect 8(a) Contractor Combating Fraud

Pbs.org/weta/thewest/resources/archieve/two/worcestr.htm

MarshallJohnWorcesterVGeorgiaArchieveofthewest @2001thewestfilmProjectandweta6 may2005

Cuny.edu/portal-ur/content/freedom-curriculum/pdf

Historyisaweapon.com

Marchand.ucdavis.edu/lessons/Cherokee/Cherokee.html

Cherokee Nation, Oklahoma

New York Times, December 2006

Small Business Administration

American Small Business League

The Cherokee Nation

Encyclopedia of American Business History

Bid Protests: The Costs are Real, But the Benefits
Outweigh Them, Daniel I. Gordon